BIGGER LOVE

HOW TO HAVE THE LOVE OF YOUR LIFE FOR THE REST OF YOUR LIFE

BY PATRICK AND SAM CULLINANE

BIGGER LOVE

by Patrick and Sam Cullinane

Copyright © 2017 by Patrick and Samantha Cullinane

Published by NoBS Music Inc.
1514 Beck Ave Suite A
Cody, WY 82414-3921

ISBN-10: 1548298115
ISBN-13: 978-1548298111

Published By NoBS Music inc.

en·deav·or

Verb

Definition: To try hard to DO or achieve something.

Synonyms: seek, undertake, aspire, aim, set out

Bigger Love takes endeavor. There is no endeavor worthier than love.

Welcome to your Love Endeavor!

TABLE OF CONTENTS

PREFACE

Patrick and I have a friend named Goose. He is a very interesting man. To meet him you might think he was homeless, and our guess is he goes through stints of homelessness as he ebbs and flows through the struggles of his life.

He rides a bike with a trailer, usually sports a Utilikilt, and he can often be found dumpster diving—it's one of his favorite hobbies. He has some medical issues that have led him down the path of substance abuse, and his personal life is strewn with many tragedies that have left him primarily alone and with a deep sorrow that can be palpably felt by those in his presence. Goose is also a Mensa member, meaning he is one of the most intelligent people on the planet.[1]

One day I had him up to the house to help out with some yard work, and we got into some absorbing conversation. "What do you think is the meaning of life?" I asked him. Goose looked up from his work and looked into my eyes and very matter-of-factly told me,

---

1   Mensans test within the upper two percent of the population for IQ.

"Love. It's love, of course."

Of course? Here was a man who had been stripped of almost all love in his life telling me he still believed it was the meaning of life. He went on further to say, "Life is tricky that way. Almost everything in the world works against it. There are so many hurdles to overcome to get to love, but then I guess that is what makes it so damn special."

So there you have it. Perhaps the meaning of life is love. To the extent that the meaning of life is the purpose of life or what makes life worthwhile, we believe love is essential. Our love, not only for each other but for ourselves, our parents, children, friends, and life itself, brings us not only our greatest moments of pleasure and joy but also our greatest challenges pushing us to growth. Love has become the major reason we do almost anything. You may not agree with us, but it is difficult to argue that love isn't something very special we seek as human beings in this life—even if it means overcoming difficult or painful obstacles to do so.

We wrote this book to help you jump some of the hurdles life may throw your way to give and receive love as best you can, with whomever you love. You may be happy and fulfilled in your current relationship, and you picked up this book because you know you can always get better, go deeper, and grow your love further. Or you may be at a crossroad. You may not be happy in your relationship anymore and might be thinking about calling it quits; you may be feeling stuck in the relationship doldrums and are seeking relief. Maybe you want to bring the spice back to your relationship.

Whatever your reasons, we hope you are here to learn, to improve, to *endeavor* to be better. We want you to be able to say, beyond a shadow of a doubt, that you have given it your absolute all because we believe no one should walk away from a significant relationship—especially a marriage—until they can say that. Whether you find yourself seeking to rediscover your love, passion, and romance, just need a tune up, or if you are just here to learn more, keep reading.

But a word of warning: If you are no longer willing to work on your relationship, then I will save you some time. Put this book down; it's not for you. Be certain to ask yourself this one question before you go: By walking away, what good will I take with me into my next relationship? Barring abusive relationships, if things aren't working now in your current relationship, it's likely as much about you as the other person. If you don't figure out your part in a failed relationship, it's likely you'll continue to repeat the negative cycles. Maybe you should keep reading? It may shed some light on what went wrong and how to take a different approach the next go round.

If we didn't piss you off with the warning, we have great news: You don't need to read fifty relationship books to get yours on track! Nor do you need to overwhelm yourself with knowledge and strategies to get your relationship in sync. You only need a few key mindsets and a few new behaviors. But it will take work. The strategies we'll discuss in these pages are simple to do but challenging to master. No one is perfect, and you likely will not be either. But, if you work at it consistently you will see a significant change for the better and likely have a relationship you might not have thought possible.

We believe that by implementing the tools and suggestions in this book, we can keep the divorce rate under ten percent. That's thirty to forty percent less than the national average (according to multiple sources of an estimated forty-to-fifty-percent divorce rate[2]). It's a very bold statement, we know. But the reason we say that is because we know from experience how great marriage can be if you have the right tools in place and are willing to do what it takes to move forward in your Love Endeavor.

ONE QUICK DISCLAIMER

This book is written as HE SAID, SHE SAID, as Sam and I offer up our individual perspectives. We're not sure if our gender or sexual orientation is relevant to this book or not—we don't think so. We're not trying to offer male/female-specific stances, nor are we speaking only to heterosexual couples. We believe that any romantic

---

2   http://www.apa.org/topics/divorce/,

partnership, regardless of the sexual orientation of those partners, can benefit from implementing the endeavors in this book.

We also need you to know that we are just normal people; we're not PhDs; we are not psychologists; we have not been studying millions of relationships for ump-teen years. We are just one of the happiest married couples we know, and we work very hard to stay that way. We weren't always happy, but we've figured out a few things, and it feels selfish not to share what we've learned with the world.

(Plus, this book offers us a little bit of a shortcut. We've had many friends ask us for relationship advice, so now reading our book will be a prerequisite to any of our unofficial marriage counseling sessions.)

Finally, we've got to warn you: there will be some colorful language sprinkled throughout this book. Mostly the S-word, but the F-word or variations of it may pop up as well. Since this book was intended for adults, we chose to write it exactly as if we were having a one-on-one conversation with you. And sometimes we swear. That's just how it is.

INTRODUCTION

OUR STORY: THE CONDENSED VERSION OF HOW WE GOT HERE

HE SAID:

It took me about a month to realize that I was dating the woman I wanted to marry. Too soon right? Probably. But I had been "interviewing" women for the previous year or two and was done being single. So when Sam came along, it was a no-brainer for me. She was different in so many ways from the rest.

I didn't want to scare Sam off, but I did want to be around her as much as I could, so I remodeled her parents' condo in my spare time. However, given that I was the first to fall madly in love, I knew I had to try and play it cool until I could get her on the same page. That took almost three months. I pulled out all stops on Valentine's

Day, which prompted the first "I love you" from her. Of course being a typical man, I said something like, "I guess I do too." Meanwhile, in my head, I was screaming, "YESSSS! What the hell took so long??"

About a month later I was sitting on the edge of her bed, and we were discussing kids. Like with so many things, we were on the same page. We both wanted kids while we were still young so that we wouldn't be changing diapers in our forties. Sam mentioned she thought I would be a good dad. She also said, in a thinking-out-loud kind of way more than she was trying to prompt me, "I won't have another kid till I get married, though." Being the opportunist I am, I charged through that door with one of the most unromantic wedding proposals ever:

"Well let's just get married then."

I was so matter-of-fact about it. I'm not sure I was even looking at her. But Sam didn't seem to notice and said, "Yeah. Okay."

We were both stone sober, but still woke up the next morning with an "Oh shit, what did I do?" feeling. When I glanced at Sam, she looked like she was struggling to comprehend our actions as well. Few words were spoken as we moved to brush our teeth. I decided I had to be the one to break the silence. With a mouthful of toothpaste foam, looking at myself in the mirror (again, not at her) I casually asked, "Did we decide to get married last night?"

Sam replied with "I .... think so ..." We both looked at each other and smiled sheepishly, but neither of us suggested further questioning. It was more like "Huh. Well, okay then."

Three months later we were married on the sunbaked red shores of Lake Powell, Utah, with about forty friends and family in attendance and the Reverend E.H Snyder III (Sam's dad, recently ordained by mail) conducting the ceremony.

While I don't necessarily recommend a six-month courtship-to-marriage plan, I won't discourage it either. There are just some things you won't learn until you have made the commitment and are experiencing the everyday fray. As an entrepreneur who has had multiple business partners, I can tell you that the courtship and the honeymoon are rarely safaris where you see the elusive animal called "true colors." That takes some time and usually won't happen until both of you attain a certain level of comfort and security.

For Sam and me, the first year was incredible, but being young and ignorant we didn't know it could get even better. Unfortunately for us, marriage was one of those things that had to get worse before it could get better. For me, it was somewhere in year two where I started having second thoughts and began asking myself if I would be able to hang in for the long haul. Most of it was between my ears and was quickly fixed after I had my first epiphany. It had to do with passion, or lack thereof, something I will talk about later. The correction I made turned things 180 degrees for me, and we were back on track but not out of the woods by any stretch.

There is a transition that happens in most relationships where the "madly in love" feeling goes away. You will read a lot more about this in upcoming chapters. Suffice to say, however, this transition is a major crossroads that is difficult to navigate without a map. We had no map and no idea what to do, as most couples don't. We winged it. Probably because we were young and smart and didn't need any help.

Years one through five were all spent in Kansas City, Missouri. That is where we really cut our teeth in our relationship. We had some ups and downs and fumbled through the transition semi successfully. We were still in love and our relationship was still pretty solid. I recognized later I had some insecurity issues that had popped up a few times and then ducked back under the surface before any real damage was done. These issues manifested as jealousy most of the time and I will fill you in on that part later. It gets its own chapter.

Sam and I didn't fight a lot but when we did it was usually about the same things. We bickered a lot about household chores and spending quality time. Sam is big on work share inside the house but gives little credit to work done outside the house. So even if I spent eight hours mowing our ten acres or rototilling our garden or building a deck off the back of the house, I would usually catch shit for not picking up after the kids or throwing in a load of laundry. Basic marriage stuff, right?

Now came the major shift. Year six we moved back to Salt Lake City, Utah. A few years prior to the move, I was a hired as a regional manager and partial owner of a company that was then acquired by UPS. So when we left Kansas City I was leaving a pretty secure gig. We moved because Sam wanted to be near her family again. She took a pay cut to move back and we took a cost of living increase. And now I was out of a job, as UPS had no need for my position in Salt Lake. I was able to scramble and replace my salary for the first six months or so, but then I was switched to commission only and I took a dip. A few months later I took another job with some equity guarantees and my salary spiked back up again. Less than a year later I would be taken advantage of and walk away empty handed. Needless to say, I was up and down with the amount of bacon I was bringing home in Utah.

Sam had taken a job working with an outsourcing company in project management. She had to drive out a month early to begin the job while I finished up mine and handled the movers in Kansas City. This was a long time apart for us. My insecurity was likely at a peak as she met new friends and went out with all of her new (all male) coworkers.

Sam has always been a fast riser at every job she has had. She moves from co-worker to upper management quicker than anyone I have seen. With this new job, the higher up she moved, the more travel they seemed to dump on her. And while I rode the income roller coaster, her income just kept climbing. So now we had a growing income gap, a work environment not conducive to an insecure husband, and travel—lots of travel. This was where our lack of tools really began to take its toll. We had no idea how to cope with the additional strain on our relationship or what to do to reduce it.

In year eight I began working with a start-up. It was again with a guarantee of equity, this time in writing, but only after we grew a profit. During the first year, no one would make any income. I still had income from another business that I had and it kept me about where I had been, but it required maybe fifteen hours a month. So most of my time was spent building equity in the new company. Or, as Sam put it: "working for free."

That year was our toughest year ever. It ultimately resulted in our separation. I had seen it coming. I did not want it however and had made a few last-ditch efforts to resurrect our marriage. One of which was to set aside some money and book us a sailing trip in the British Virgin Islands over the kids' spring break. This backfired badly. Sam never knew how much I made because she focused on averages and the tax return black and white. In my other business I didn't make much for the first six months of the year, but it started really ramping up after that and in November and December I usually made half of my annual income. That December I had made more than any other, and setting a few thousand aside for the "surprise" trip was easy.

Well Sam hated that surprise and accused me of hiding money. Fuck. We went on the trip and had a pretty good time with the kids, but our conversations all seemed to have an element of finality to them. What I mean by that is we talked a lot on this trip about what was wrong, and each time we seemed further apart and sad. Two months later, Sam suggested we take some time apart. I found an apartment a few miles away the next day.

I may have been able to beg and suggest counseling and gone the usual route, but I tended to own things and to react with emotion. My emotions were hurt and anger, and they manifested themselves with this kind of dialogue: "Fuck her. I won't be where I am not wanted." "She wants to be on her own? Good, now she will see how much help I was really giving." "If she thinks there is someone better out there, good luck keeping that person when he realizes the kind of shit he is dealing with." "She took a knee on the one yard line; my businesses are just getting ready to pay off!" And they were.

I focused on my business and that kind of internal dialogue for about five months. At that time I was in North Idaho visiting my terminally ill cousin and dear friend. I believe it was also around this time that my other cousin Dan gave me a much needed verbal bitch slap. "Why don't you stop focusing on everything Sam did wrong and why this is mostly her fault? he said. "Instead focus on your part in all of this. You have your own shit. Whether you get back together or not, do you want to haul that baggage with you into the next relationship?"

That was a huge moment for me and likely led to another epiphany. I had heard it my whole life but never really knew what it meant until right then. I only have control over so much. Sam and her decisions are definitely not part of it. I need to focus on what I can control which is me, and I have some work to do. I decided practically on the spot that my own insecurity was as much at fault as anything else and I would start changing that now.

Another thing Dan said was: "You need to stop owning her shit. You own it for days." I will expand much more on this in a later chapter. But let me say that not long after that conversation with Dan I stopped letting Sam's moods, her perceptions and her misplaced values be something that I would let bother me.

We did have one major blowup over Christmas, but not many more after that because I refused to fall back into my old patterns. Our fight over Christmas was of course about money, which for some reason made me defensive. The divorce papers were being drawn up. In them I got zero credit for signing the house over to her. That's what I get for refusing to have a lawyer and basically telling her she could have everything except my tools, my car, our log bed I built, and of course my baseball cards. I digress.

She was mad at this time because her lawyer told

her that our tax returns showed that I only needed to pay $300.00 a month in child support. Forgetting everything I was working on and allowing myself to be sucked in, I shot back "You said you make all the money, you said you don't need me, you said you wanted to be on your own, so what difference does it make what the child support number is?" Yeah, that helped.

A week later I called her and said, "I don't want to have the same conversation we had last week. So how about this, I know you don't need money to take care of the kids when you have them, and I will pay when I do. So the child support number is somewhat meaningless. And we should just leave it as is in the paperwork and not fight about it. Additionally, I will deposit $1,000.00 a month into their college fund. I have already given you everything else, so my word will have to be good here. I will start by dropping in ten K in January to prepay February and one thousand for every month we have been apart."

I think this might be when she realized I was not the broke dick she had been portraying me as in her own internal and external dialogue. My business had started paying a decent salary a month or so after we split. I also was teed up for regular equity splits starting in January. On top of that, my other business had a great last quarter as always. I had finally turned the corner. It felt really good to defuse the money argument with money for a change. This was likely the shedding of one of my last major insecurities.

The new me had evolved into a person who had found success, didn't show insecurities such as jealousy, did not engage in blowups or shit that had little to do with me, and finally knew that I would be happy either with or without her. I think Sam was attracted to the new me all over again. In May of that year, I invited her to a massage and a sleepover. She accepted. That night we decided to get back together.

The truth is I never stopped loving Sam, and I had continued holding out some hope we could reconcile. And when we agreed to give it another try, I was elated. We had conditions for each other though and these conditions were critical to how it came to be. Mine were that she needed to recognize that her job consumed her and that she was being manipulated and taken advantage of by the people she worked with. Fortunately for me she already had connected those dots and wanted to quit after the summer. That was huge for me as I knew that if she prioritized our family over her job, we would not fail again.

I also suggested she not go back to work for a while after she quit. She agreed and said we would play it by ear. Aside from a few small projects with her dad and working in our own business, I am proud to say she has never gone back to work for another person. If she wants to, I will support her as my only goal is for her to be happy. But I also know that's not what makes her happy.

I am forever grateful too because she saved my ass more than once by being free to help grow our own business.

The last ten years of our relationship have been nothing short of spectacular. The love continues to grow, expand and flourish and our foundation is more solid than ever. It has not been perfect, nothing ever is. But we are still keen to learn and continue to do so. Much of this book is about what we have learned since our "almost divorce" and how we integrated that knowledge to help us even further.

SHE SAID:

Patrick (or Paddy, as I lovingly call him) and I met in 1995 at a party. The parents of my best friend Nicole (or Nickel, as I lovingly call her) were hosting a holiday party at their house. Paddy was a friend of Nickel's, but that night he was there with a group that had come to hang out with her parents. Nickel's parents were and are young at heart, so their parties brought together a wide variety of people of all ages and interests.

Paddy is seven years older than me, which seemed like a big age difference at the time and that bothered me to begin with. However, we hit it off immediately, and his gentle, loving ways combined with his unrelenting persistence soon had me smitten.

I wasn't the only one who'd fallen for Paddy—my two-year-old son Jacob **loved** him. Paddy would greet

Jacob with as much enthusiasm as he greeted me and they seemed to really enjoy playing together. Soon my son was just as excited to see Paddy as I was. When Christmas came, Paddy bought him a giant stuffed Pumba (the warthog from *The Lion King* and Jacob's favorite character in his favorite movie) with bugs you could take in and out of his mouth. This thing was about as big as Jacob, and he loved it.

Having Jacob and Paddy love each other was hugely important to me. I wanted a loving family who wanted to spend time together. Finding a partner who loved my son as much as, or more than he loved me, seemed the only way to do this. I had dated men who were only interested in me as a partner and not me as a mother. This caused conflict as these men were always angling to exclude Jacob and I was always toting him along. I didn't want my love for my child to be compromised by my love for a partner—I wanted to be both a happy partner and mother all at the same time.

After three months of dating, we started talking about having another child together. I didn't want Jacob to be an only child and be left here on earth alone when I passed away. (I know what you're thinking: *That's a little morbid and premature for a twenty-two-year-old*, but what can I say? I'm an old soul.) I also didn't want the age gap between my kids to be so big that they wouldn't be close. Being a single mother was very difficult, and I wanted someone who was committed to helping me raise my kids. And to me, that meant being married. So Paddy and I decided to tie the knot. It was an abrupt decision, and it shocked us both when we suggested it, discussed it and then agreed to it.

I remember when I told Nickel that I was getting married, she responded with "To who?" I suppose it was a fair question. I'd been trying to play the field and had dated a few other guys for the first few months I was seeing Paddy. In fact, Paddy even babysat Jacob while I went on a date with another man! (That was part of the unrelenting persistence I mentioned earlier.) We had a very short whirlwind romance; we got hitched; we moved from Park City to Kansas City, Missouri, and had our daughter, Claire, a year later. We lived in Kansas City for a little over five years.

Our marriage through those first five years, although not perfect, was satisfactory. We weren't without our struggles, adjustments, fighting, and discontentment but we managed to stumble through without too much damage—or so we thought—but some resentment was starting to build up.

Paddy is an entrepreneur. He thrives in environments where he calls his own shots and paves his own way. During the first half our marriage, Paddy's moneymaking activities felt like a roller coaster ride of different side jobs, start-ups, partnerships, and experiments. I, on the other hand, was a corporate woman. My grandfather and father both had great success in the corporate world so I followed suit with what I knew. My career was a steady climb up the corporate ladder, providing our family with what I thought was stability and financial security.

In 2001, we started discussing moving back to Utah. My grandparents were aging and I wanted to be around to spend time with them before they passed on. Paddy graciously agreed. I found another corporate job and Paddy also secured a venture he could pursue in Utah.

My new job required extensive travel and Paddy primarily worked from home. I would often leave town early Monday morning and return late on Friday evening or Saturday morning. We frequently pulled late and all-nighters to meet deadlines and took red-eye flights so we could get home before heading back out on the road. I would typically arrive home exhausted to a messy house, piles of laundry, kids needing baths, hair combing, and other motherly TLC—and a husband needing attention and other wifely TLC.

This put tremendous strain on me and subsequently our relationship. I often used what little energy I had over the weekends to clean, do the laundry, get in as much time with the kids as possible, and Paddy got whatever I might have left—if anything. My priorities in those days were: number one, providing for our family; number two, the kids; and Paddy came in last.

I was also building resentment towards Paddy. I felt like since I was the main financial provider for our family and Paddy was home, he could at least clean up and do laundry. I was also critical of the way he took care of our children. He didn't bathe them as regularly as I would have, they didn't eat as well as I would have fed them, and my husband let them dress themselves and comb their own hair. Seeing Claire come home from school in her dress-up Cinderella garb made me feel embarrassed and it would take multiple sessions of crying and hair combing to work out the rat's nest at the back of her neck each weekend—she only brushed the top part.

Then there was the unending male attention I received at work. When I started my job in Utah, I was the only woman in my entire division who was not an administrative assistant. I was often the only woman working on my teams, and many of my male colleagues became close friends. As I spent less and less time at home with Paddy, I found the time I did spend with him more draining than pleasurable. As I spent more time traveling with those colleagues, some of those friendships teetered on the line of crushes, and a few tipped over into the realm of emotional affairs.

I was getting all the male attention I could ever want—short of sex (which as you'll read about later in this book, wasn't a high priority for me). So because it wasn't physical, I didn't consider this to be cheating, technically. This is not what I believe now. I believe emotional affairs to be as damaging as physical affairs but the lines aren't as clear.

My job had many perks—always traveling first

class or in private planes, limos, five-star hotels, and conferences and meetings in exotic locations like the Caribbean and Europe. I also received expensive gifts such as jewelry from Tiffany's, a Tag Heuer watch, and thousands of dollars of gift certificates to Nordstrom's for holidays and birthdays, or bonuses for closing big deals. I was being exposed to an entirely different world—the lap of luxury.

I started to feel like, why can't I have a husband who wears a suit, works a stable corporate job, buys me a new car for Christmas (one of my male colleagues had bought his wife a very expensive car for Christmas!)? Why do I have to be the stable provider? I loved my job but I also missed my kids and would often cry as my flights left Utah.

I tried a few things to relieve the pressure and create more space for family. We hired an amazing nanny, Mel, who lived across the street with her partner, Sean, and their two children who were the same ages as our kids. Although this helped with many of the household duties, it actually seemed to throw gas on the fire of my resentment towards Paddy. Now not only was I working extremely hard, but my husband who was working from home was either unable or unwilling to tend to our household and children, which meant I had to pay someone else to do it. And Paddy brought in some income but I brought in more than double and I felt like I was working at least twice as hard.

I started wondering, what did I need a husband for anyway? Our sex life had degraded to nearly nothing, as I felt little to no attraction to Paddy, who seemed uninterested in anything but hounding me for sex and attention and riding my ass about being distant. I got all of my emotional support from friends and male colleagues. I paid a nanny to take care of my children and my household. I didn't need his income to support my lifestyle—and in fact I felt cutting ties would help my financial situation because I'm a saver and Paddy is a spender which also caused tension.

We spent about three years muddling through life this way until I decided being married to Paddy was more trouble than it was worth. Just a month before our tenth anniversary I told him I was done. We had a brief discussion of what to do with our assets and Paddy said I could have them all—the house, the car, our retirement account—everything. He would essentially be leaving with nothing but his car.

Shortly thereafter, I was offered a position in Spain and told him I would like to move our children to Europe with me. I felt it was an opportunity of a lifetime for all of us. My company would fly Paddy out every few months to visit the kids, which would also be a great opportunity for him. He also thought this would be an amazing experience for our kids. They would be able to learn another language or two, see another culture, and he agreed to the move.

So we were done. I met with a lawyer and started the process of getting divorced, moved to Spain with our children, rented out my house in Utah to friends, and started my new life where the grass would be greener.

My job in Spain was dramatically different from the positions I held in the States. I was essentially hired to clean up a giant multi-million-dollar mess our company was making there. I led a very large team spread all over Europe and was working with mostly new people. Almost immediately upon my arrival I could feel a new sort of loneliness of being THE boss and also an outsider—an American—oh, and again, one of the only women on our management team.

I'd had the impression my job would require little to no travel, which appealed to me. I thought I could be with my children more. We rented a little condo right on the sea in a beautiful medieval town named Sitges and I enrolled them in the international school. I chose this town partially because when I went there one night with some people from work, there were gorgeous men everywhere and I thought these would be great hunting grounds for my new singleness. (I later found out Sitges is the unofficial gay capital of Europe. Whoops!)

Paddy came to visit the kids after those first couple months. I told him he could stay in our condo and I figured he could be in charge of the kids for the week since I was again traveling and struggling to find reliable help. I was surprised by how happy I was to see him. My first few months on the greener grass had been nothing short of intense. The job was extremely difficult and demanding—I wasn't seeing my children as much as I had hoped—I had only two friends, Linda and Keith from Canada, but no time or outlets to find new friends. I was lonely and the familiarity of Paddy was comforting.

We hadn't had an ugly parting of ways, it was friendly and we spoke often about the kids and how to handle different things. I hadn't had sex with anyone since I left him and although we had sex infrequently, I missed being touched and after a few months I did start missing sex.

The plan was for Paddy to sleep on the couch but he snuck into my room the first or second night and we talked and touched and had sex. He was still as gentle, loving, and persistent as when we met. It didn't feel right but it didn't feel wrong either. It didn't mean we were getting back together but it was a nice respite from my new lonely life.

My big plans for my new life started to fall apart after three months. My company was unable to secure visas for my children to legally live in Spain any longer. The government of Barcelona wasn't extending these visas to anyone and none of our team could get them pushed through. Jacob and Claire had to leave the country while they tried to sort out the visa issues. I took the kids and our new awesome Spanish nanny, Alvaro, to work out of our office in London for a month hoping my team could work something out in the meantime. The visas didn't get done and the kids and I went home for Christmas.

My stay at home for Christmas was extended. I stayed with my parents and went into our office where they had set up a new, fancy video conferencing system for me to use to run my team from Utah while we sorted out the visa issues. I would arrive to work at the office around midnight when my teams were starting their days, home around noon, bed by five, repeat. I got to see the kids a few hours in the afternoons and every other weekend. And I was always exhausted.

I realized a couple things over Christmas. I found my former crushes and emotional affairs had dissolved to close to nothingness in my absence—they had been fleeting encounters with those feelings of being in love. I had been dumped in Europe in the biggest sinking boat of a business with little of the promised support that was to be provided from my former teams. I was now going to be seeing even less of my children than before I took the assignment without their visas. And my company had already found my replacement to do my former job, so there was no turning back at this point.

One night Paddy and I had dinner. According to our not-quite-final divorce he would need to pay child support since I had custody of the kids. It turned into a big fight over $300 a month, which I didn't need at all and since the divorce wasn't final he didn't think he needed to pay. I drove home bawling in hysterics.

I had no idea why I was crying until I reached my parents' house.

I suddenly realized I was extremely unhappy and I had reached this place because of Paddy. It was his fault that I had to be the big provider because he never stepped up. So that also made it his fault that I hated my new job. It was his fault I was lonely. It was his fault I missed my kids and had missed so much of their childhood—it was all because he had never given me a chance to stay home with my kids.

But the real epiphany ... the real message in that anger had nothing to do with Paddy at all. The real message was I only thought I wanted a big career and to travel the world and have expensive things. But deep down I didn't give a shit about any of that. I missed my kids—I wanted to be with them and see them grow up and take care of them and learn how to cook. The real message in the sorrow was that I had wasted so many years chasing shiny things and empty fleeting feelings masked as financial stability. When I had graduated from college with a degree in international relations, I honestly imagined my life as being the big boss living as an expat with a full-time nanny. Turns out I had arrived and it wasn't anything I really wanted.

And Paddy seemed to be getting his financial shit together. Maybe all those years of roller coaster entrepreneurialism were starting to pay off? He lived in a nice apartment, he had just bought a new Land Rover, and for Christmas he bought me beautiful diamond earrings. I ended up spending the night at his new apartment and we slept together again. Again, it was so comforting and he was still just as gentle, loving, and persistent as ever. He also proposed after our big fight that in lieu of child support—which we both knew I didn't need—he would put $1,000 in the kids' college funds every month. Again, it wasn't about the material things—the diamond earrings or the Land Rover—but it was more a display that Paddy didn't really need to rely on me financially. He was making his own way just fine and maybe better than fine.

On my next trip home, Paddy asked me on an official date for dinner and a night at Snowbird lodge. I figured since we had been sleeping together the whole time we were getting divorced, it was likely I would put out after a date, so the overnight sounded good to me. It wasn't like I was seeing anyone else.

We had an amazing night. Paddy told me confidently that night, "I will be fine—happy—with or without you." I had never heard anything so sexy in my life! I had always felt this burden of his reliance on me—of our family reliance on me—real or not—and the burden lifted immediately. Not unlike our whirlwind romance when we first got married, we decided to get back together that very night. I told Paddy I hated my job and wanted to quit. He told me his business was booming and he would love it if I quit my job and we all moved home.

I planned my exit—hiring two people who were each paid twice what I was making—to replace me. I always knew I was doing the job of at least two people and underpaid as a woman. Before my complete exit, Paddy and I took the kids on an awesome vacation through the North of Spain—staying in castles, playing in the ocean, and enjoying the beautiful Spanish countryside, food, and culture.

Once we got home, while we were at a party at my sister's house with all of our friends, Paddy got down on one knee with a gorgeous antique diamond ring and proposed to me. We had an all-Elvis re-wedding in Vegas with all of our friends and we've truly lived "Happily Ever After" ever since.

If I had to summarize—why did we break up in the first place?

I put my career before anything or anyone in my life. I allowed my job to be my number one priority. I justified this choice by stating I was supporting my family, but in truth my job gave me lots of things, including more money than I really needed to support my family. It brought instant gratification—money, power, prestige, gifts, trips, luxuries. It gave me lots of positive attention. Unfortunately, none of these things last, nor are they important to me personally. I'm happier drinking a Bud Light in a camping chair in the desert than I am dressed to the nines sipping Champagne at the Ritz-Carlton. I'm especially happier if my kids and husband are there!

I put my career before anything or anyone in my life. I know I'm repeating myself but I put my career even before myself. When I was working that hard, I was not taking care of myself. I ate poorly, I was out of shape, I didn't sleep enough, and my stress levels were through the roof. I practiced zero self-love and when you don't take care of yourself, as I showed, you have nothing left for anyone else.

I didn't know myself well enough, or I chose to ignore the things that are truly important to me. Jacob, Claire, and Paddy are the most important things in my life. They are why I do anything. I lost sight of this and it nearly cost me everything.

Now if I have to summarize—why did I *want* to get back together with Paddy?

The sex was amazing. Paddy is a great lover. I trained him well. It would likely take years to train anyone else to love me like he does because I'd been training him for years.

Paddy had new ... swagger? Paddy had this confidence when we met—he told me, "I'll be a millionaire one day, Sam. I promise you that." It had waned while my career soared and his took a bit of a digger, but during our year apart he got his swagger back. He was confident again. That was hot.

Paddy loves our kids as much as I do. What do I love the most on this planet? Jacob and Claire. I fucking love those kids more than anything. And having that much love for something and knowing someone else has that much love for something is bonding. It can't carry a partnership but if you let it, it can strengthen one.

Many people say we're very lucky, but we would tell you luck has nothing to do with it. We work on our marriage. We nurture it to make it what it is today. And much of that effort is dedicated to working on who we are as human beings, communicating with one another, and expressing love. The things we've learned along the way (which we've included in these pages) make the work of our marriage easier, more fulfilling, and deeper. We can't wait to share them with you.

Who would you say is the love of your life?

Answer: _____

CHAPTER 1

THE LOVE OF YOUR LIFE

If you didn't say yourself, you need to start rethinking your answer!

According to Aristotle, "All friendly feelings for others are an extension of a man's feelings for himself."

You are the love of your life. You are the only one who really knows you, who has been and will be with you every moment of your life from the cradle to the grave. It seems trite to say, but self-love is a vital aspect of your ability to love someone else. Your ability to love, feel gratitude for, and forgive yourself teaches you how to express those things to others.

That said, we believe achieving complete self-love is right up there with achieving total enlightenment. Sure, some people reach it, but most of us stumble along the path doing our best to find something we know is elusive. We feel it is more helpful to describe self-love as a process as opposed to a destination, so we don't become discouraged.

We are not self-love experts but having seen glimpses of how our relationship flourishes when we are practicing self-love, we work our asses off on a daily basis to get just a bit further down that path.

SHE SAID: WHY LOVE YOURSELF AND HOW DO YOU GET THERE?

In those years where our marriage started to degrade before our almost-divorce, I practiced very little (if any) self-love. If I made mistakes, particularly in business, I would beat myself up for days, months even. I had zero compassion for screw-ups. I thought to get sick was weakness and popped pills to take care of the symptoms and tried to ignore them. If I had successes, I spent very little time celebrating them before moving on to the next task or project. This is how I treated myself—it was also how I treated Paddy, Jacob, Claire, and I took that to another level with every soul who had the misfortune of reporting to me. I was brutal, first on myself and then on others.

I ate and drank whatever I wanted whenever I wanted, which I can tell you involved a diet of primarily caffeine, sugar, alcohol, and popcorn with an occasional swanky dinner at an expensive restaurant. I sacrificed sleep to finish work, meet deadlines, or party with co-workers.

"Sleep when you are dead" was something of a mantra. I never exercised—who had time for that?

I was attempting some spiritual life and took up Zen Buddhism, but I only practiced when I was at home—which was rarely—and when I was home, I primarily volunteered and taught the kids' class as a service to the Zen Center as opposed to engaging in my own practice. I had given up all hobbies.

I had very few friends. I was under extreme pressure to perform and in the spotlight. My job got all of me, and I thought I really loved it and the perks. I thought I was fulfilled.

But there were indicators everything wasn't peachy.

I left nothing for anything or anyone else. I told my children "no" to many of the things they asked for such as sleepovers, parties, and excursions because I didn't have the energy to facilitate them. I was also not very affectionate—I wasn't raised in an overly affectionate family, and honestly, I preferred not to be touched too much.

Every vacation we took during those years, I would get really sick to the point of not being able to leave a hotel room for the first few days no matter how many pills I popped. I preferred to sleep than go on excursions with my family. When we were in the Caribbean sailing through the Virgin Islands, Paddy, Jacob, and Claire went snorkeling, and I decided to take a nap.

I cried in the car on the way to work almost every

morning and on every flight leaving Utah.

The long-term effects of not practicing self-love were the near demise of my marriage; having children who heard the words "I love you" all the time but didn't really see or feel me expressing love towards them; health issues I still battle whose causes are rooted in not taking care of my body during all those years along with the side effects of not properly managing stress and anxiety. Thankfully, I learned my lesson:

You practice self-care as a form of self-love. You place the oxygen mask on yourself first before helping others.

Here are a few ways to implement more self-care and self-love into your life.

Self-love means taking care of your body.

We take care of our bodies, so we'll feel good and live a long time! This means eating and drinking healthy and being educated and intentional about what you are putting in your body as fuel. It means moving your body. Our bodies are made to move, and your health will plummet if you are too sedentary. Exercise is also an excellent way to manage stress and anxiety.

Self-care involves seeking out healthcare professionals when things aren't feeling right or going well, and not waiting too long to do it. It means flossing and going to the dentist so you can keep your teeth.

Self-love means taking care of your mind and your spirit.

What do you love? What activities light you up, exhilarate you, or make you excited? What would you do right now if you could do anything in the world?

Doing things that bring you joy is critical to self-love. It feeds your mind and your spirit. There were a few years there where, when we had free time, I would let everyone in my family decide what we would do. Paddy loves sports so I'd end up at a tailgate and a football game. The kids love going out to eat, movies, and they both like bowling, so those were often family activities.

Then there are the things that I do for myself. I love being outdoors—hiking, skiing, camping. I love writing songs and playing music. I love dancing. I make time for the things that bring me joy. When I light up from doing something I love it's contagious and tends to spread and light up the people around me. I show up in the world the way I want the world to show up for me: enthusiastic, excited, joyful. And when you show up that way, your expressions of love for other people are more easily seen and felt. Try it. You'll see what I'm talking about. You wouldn't deny the people you love doing the things that bring them joy, so don't deny yourself that privilege either.

Without getting too religious or preachy, engaging in spiritual practice is a part of self-love too. Allowing, growing, or pursuing a connection to something larger than yourself can feed your soul, bring you peace, reduce your stress—all of which enable you to bring a better self to any relationship. I'm not religious, but I do have a spiritual practice and I meditate every day. It carries not only a spiritual benefit but also focus, clarity, and improved brainwave activity.[3]

Fostering self-love as an emotion is hard work but will likely show the most immediate results in your relationships.

Our ability to love anyone or anything, including ourselves, lies in our ability to focus on and appreciate all of the good stuff, accept the flaws, and forgive the mistakes. Learn to do this for yourself, and you can do it for your partner.

Squash self-criticism.

As I mentioned earlier, I used to spend quite a bit of time beating myself up for my mistakes. I would think about the mistake and turn it all around in my mind as a type of "post-mortem" while criticizing myself for being so dumb, naïve, lazy, or any number of negative qualities I may have displayed at the time of making the error. I would relive those moments over and over again in my mind.

How do you think I felt about myself while I relived my mistakes in my head and called myself all of those negative things? Good? Happy? Ready to take on the world? Of course not. It was more like self-loathing and wondering how I managed to do anything well.

---

3   https://www.washingtonpost.com/news/inspired-life/wp/2015/05/26/harvard-neuroscientist-meditation-not-only-reduces-stress-it-literally-changes-your-brain/

I used to let my mind go wherever it wanted, think whatever it wanted and believe every thought. Don't fall into the trap of believing all your own thoughts. Just because you have them doesn't make them real. You get to choose if they are true or not. "I made a big mistake" is a truth, because we all make big mistakes. "I am shit because of the big mistake I made" is not true unless you decide it's true.

It's far more useful to ask, "Does that thought serve me and help me become my best and highest self? Or does that thought bring me down?" How about, "Would I ever say this to my child? Or my best friend?" If the answer is no, these are the thoughts you need to start weeding out. Paddy talks about this as negative self-talk. We both agree: Part of self-love is listening to what you are saying to yourself and start shutting down the nasty shit.

Unfortunately, this is easier said than done. You need to become more aware of your thoughts—that internal dialogue we all have in our heads. Meditation can be useful to train you to hear them and particularly a mindfulness practice. I like Unified Mindfulness[4] because it takes a more scientific approach. It takes a little time to understand the technique and some practice but luckily just ten minutes a day for a few months can bring you closer, faster. Being aware of unkind thoughts without buying into them or trying to make them go

---

4   http://unifiedmindfulness.com/

away, helps you stay focused on what really matters.

I took an online spirituality class called *A Spirit-Led Life* from an amazing human being named Jenai Lane[5] who has deepened my understanding of many of the principles we discuss in this book. In this class, we were asked to identify our "integrity holes," places where we were not in integrity with ourselves. These are the activities, thoughts, feelings that take the wind out of your sail and drain your energy. My negative self-talk and self-criticism were at the top of my list.

The exercise started out simply enough: I identified the negative self-talk and self-criticism as my integrity holes, and acknowledged that I had a tendency to judge myself critically. The next steps got a little hairier. After recognition came labeling, taking a moment to call a critical or judgmental thought what it is, then we had to "let it go," releasing that negativity through a quick meditation and forgiving myself for having these thoughts.

I set the intention to start this new activity the next morning. I get up around 5:00 AM and I start my workout at 6:15 most mornings, and I couldn't believe it when I counted over twenty critical and judgmental thoughts between when the alarm went off and when

---

5   Jenai Lane is an author and coach offering classes, seminars, and retreats that I highly recommend. http://www.spiritcoachtraining.com/ She offers a free introduction to some of her tools – some I discuss in this book (SpiritCoachTraining.com/FreeCourse) and one of my favorites work is her 5-Minute Meditation which is also on her website for free (SpiritCoachTraining.com/5Min).

it was time to exercise! I undoubtedly would have had many more, but it took a considerable amount of time to stop, label, "let go," and forgive myself in between each of these thoughts! I had to slow my critical roll if I was going to get anything done that day.

After practicing this technique for only a few days, I went from approximately one negative thought every two minutes to less than one an hour. Not too shabby.

The next step was to try to trade out my few remaining negative thoughts with something more ... gentle? Inspiring? *Self-loving.* These ended up being on-the-fly affirmations of sorts. I tried to think of what I might say to my children. So for example, one of my negative thoughts today was, "I can't believe I didn't get up at 5:00 and skipped my workout. I'm so lazy and clearly not dedicated enough." Ouch. When I caught myself thinking these things, I quickly countered that up with, "But I'll be up at 5:00 tomorrow to get back on track!" Better right? These are habits you develop over time, with practice, not quick fixes that will happen overnight.

Self-appreciation is self-love.

To achieve a higher level of self-love, I also spend a few minutes every morning making a list of things I'm grateful for and love about myself. When I started doing this, it was torture. I would sit there for thirty minutes or more. Sometimes really trying to think of things but mostly distracting myself with other thoughts or fidgeting. Sometimes this still happens, but I have pages and pages now of things I love and appreciate about myself I can refer back to in a pinch.

So what does this look like? I often start at the very most basic level. I'm grateful to be alive, to have the experience of living life as a human on the earth. So I translate that gratitude to something I'm grateful for about myself:

> *I love my soul that allows me life—for that spark that started my heart beating and my lungs to breathing. I love my body and all of its senses that enable me to experience life and the world. I love my mind that organizes all the information it receives. I love my curiosity that has allowed me to learn all I know.*

And you could go on and on with those, but then I usually try to think of what I have going on that day and what I might need to accomplish and then I try to kind of pump myself up about those things. I write and record music, so if those are the activities I'm going to be doing that day, some of my self-love lists say things like:

> *I love my creativity that brings the music. I love that my ability to learn new things has allowed me to become a recording engineer.*

You get the idea. Think of this in terms of your gifts, the things you were given when you were born. I was generalizing with "my body," but you could say, "my eyes with 20/20 vision," or, "my singing voice," or any number of other things.

Where is your focus?

What you focus on grows. If you keep your attention on all of the negative things about yourself, those things get bigger. If you concentrate on the amazing things about yourself, you'll notice those things also grow bigger, if even only in your own heart and mind. The good news is that this is really the only place that it matters anyhow.

You practice self-love to learn how to love others better.

A friend once told me he had no idea how anyone could stay in a relationship, running down a thorough list of every negative thing from his most recent love affair to prove his point. He talked about his ex's flaws, personality and physical, and their annoying habits and quirks. I listened for quite some time, doing my best to keep from criticizing or judging him for his criticisms and judgments. I said instead:

"You know, Paddy is growing more and more hair as we get older, especially in places like his ears. And he's always been gassy, except when we were dating of course. And he chews his nails. And all of his household projects take at least twice as long as he says they will."

"BUT," I added, "instead of focusing on those things, I choose to focus on his mesmerizing blue-green eyes that change colors depending on what he is wearing; on the fact that he is one of the most generous men I know; how he can fix anything, and how he gives the very best hugs."

Listen, we all have flaws. We all make mistakes. We all have our shit. IF you practice taking care of yourself, so you feel your best; IF you forgive your mistakes and flaws while reminding yourself of all of the amazing things about yourself; IF you treat these things as a practice and not a destination, you will feel the ripples of those changes to yourself emanate through all of your relationships. It is the most difficult thing for us to learn to extend ourselves these courtesies, but once we have done that, it is simple to extend them to everyone else. IF you do these things, I guarantee you will be a happier, better version of yourself. I would also bet your relationship will also reap the benefits of these changes.

Self-love, just like all love, is more than a mere emotion. It is a practice.

HE SAID: LOVE YOURSELF? WHAT THE...

It has been repeated to me over and over that, "You must first love yourself before you can become the best you possible." For most of my life, I have not really understood this principle. In the last chapter, I talked about insecurity as something that I struggled with earlier in our relationship and life and how that insecurity manifested itself. Looking back, I can see many other places insecurity popped up in my life and relationships. Insecurity, in my opinion, is the antithesis of loving oneself.

Well there you have it, my part is done. Don't be insecure, love yourself, it's that simple. Got it?

I wish it were that simple, but it's not, and I have to try to convey this point no matter how uncomfortable it is to do. Why is it uncomfortable? Because I am still a work in progress with this whole love yourself thing.

In today's media-infused society, loving yourself completely is fucking hard if not impossible. As men, we are constantly bombarded with various dick measuring contests everywhere we look. If you turn off ads, someone is junk emailing you about low T, or blue pills, whiter teeth, or hair growth. Everyone who is selling something is telling us that we are not good enough.

The message is clear: You're only good or successful if someone else thinks you are. The hot young girl slows her walk to stop, slowly turns her head and smiles seductively at the man with the new car rolling by. These messages condition us to believe that everything is validated by the opinions of others, how many "likes" or "shares" you get. None of this has anything to do with self-love; it has everything to do with insecurity. Loving yourself can be an uphill battle when the rest of society is incessantly preying on your insecurity that you are not good enough unless...

SHE SAID:

Ahem ... you really think you men have it hard with the media? Women have to have bubble butts, big tits, small waists, muscular but not too bulky legs, and we are absolutely not allowed to age or risk becoming irrelevant, where old men like Sean Connery are still sexy. Oh, and we also have to play the bimbo who is acting like the guy is somehow hot because of the car.

ENOUGH WHINING, BACK TO HE SAID:

Men, in general, are supposed to be—say it with me guys: Strong, Confident, Decisive, Successful, Hunters, Heroes. I am puffing my chest out and growling a bit right now just writing these things. Grrrrrr I am MAN!

Bullshit.

I am Patrick.

I have to start there. That is the beginning of getting on track to self-loving.

For me, there is always a little voice inside me saying I can do better. I think that voice is necessary, but I have grown to realize that I also need to be able to recognize when it is full of shit. Sometimes that voice is a product of the conditioned belief that I am not good enough, or that I won't be happy unless I have or do something else.

I am getting way better at recognizing that voice and eliminating it. But it is not easy. For example, I thought it would be cool to have a Sprinter camper van. If it was diesel, got decent mileage and was in my budget, I might want one for exploring the US. So I went to RVT.com and looked at used Sprinter vans for thirty minutes. Nothing. Okay, I don't need one to be happy because what I wanted didn't exist. Tell that to Google. I have been bombarded with ads about Sprinter vans for the last six weeks. It is incessant. These ads are really trying to condition me that I need one to be happy. It's a benign example, but it should illustrate the point of the constant bombardment by media with the sole purpose of influencing our thinking. So turn it off.

I have always had an answer to the question, "What do you love most about yourself?" but there's a big difference between being able to describe your better qualities and showing yourself love. At my core, I had been so unsatisfied with who I was, and the soundtrack playing between my ears reflected that. I was very hard on myself and rarely used kind words when looking in the mirror. Here is an example of my past usual self-talk: "I procrastinate. I need to lose fifteen pounds. I'm starting to look fat. I suck at meditating. I suck at consistent exercise. I should not be eating this food that is so bad for me."

Recently I had a moment of clarity. It came when I saw the gap between how I let others see me—a funny, life of the party, genuine person, who really cares about people—and how I saw myself. I recognized that underneath those veneers, was a guy who constantly told himself he wasn't good enough. Underneath was a guy who usually used humor to deflect the real questions he didn't want to answer.

That moment of clarity was fueled by spending two weeks on a bucket list adventure in Vietnam with GoBundance, a mastermind group I belong to. We had come together for deep conversation and to ask and answer some really tough questions, all with the goal of pushing each other to become better, more balanced men. I was talking about our book and quoted Sam by saying, "The first person you need to love in a relationship is yourself. You can't love others completely until you do that." I guess by posing the topic, I set myself up to have to answer it first. "Patrick, do you really love yourself?"

My response was, "Can you be more specific?" Then, when the chuckling subsided, I said, "Oh most definitely. In fact, I loved myself this morning—that's why there is an empty box of Kleenex and a bottle of Jergens next to the bed." Deflect. Deflect again. Then one more deflection for good measure. I then sighed and added, "You know I am not sure …" But before my moment of vulnerability could set in, I threw in one last self-protective deflection: "It's a good thing Sam is writing that chapter in our book!" Funny? I thought so, which is probably why I laughed harder than everyone else.

After I made my jokes and successfully deflected, I paused, and then I just sat there. I realized I could not answer the question. At that moment, I knew I did not accept myself completely. Therefore I did not love myself completely.

In addition to asking each other tough questions, the men of GoBundance get up in front of each other and talk about important aspects of our lives. We expose our flaws and desires to improve. We tell one another what we need the most help with and where we need accountability. I listened to several people say "my relationship" or "my exercise and nutrition." I joined the chorus and cited exercise and diet as the things I needed the most help with, too. Deflect.

Then came, "What do you love most about yourself?" I again listened to each person's answer before giving my own, saying, "I love my everyday desire to improve as a man." Bullshit.

Later on the trip (the exact moment of clarity) I sat at a table discussing self-love with another member of our tribe, and I realized the hypocrisy AND the simplicity of the whole topic. The hypocrisy was how we had accepted each other's answers to the question over and over again when it was clear that they were facades. And I was right at the forefront. The simplicity was that it ALL stemmed from the same source. Weight, exercise, relationship problems, procrastination—no matter the "topic," they all related to the exact same thing: a lack of self-love.

The question is not "What do you love most about yourself?" which can easily be answered with a shiny coat of gloss, leaving the foundation of the problem rotting away. The question—the ONLY question—should be, "Do you love yourself?" If I loved myself, would I take better care of myself? If I loved myself, would I do what I said, especially if I'd only made that promise to myself?

Here is the real mind blowing part. When I do not love myself (e.g., don't work out, eat junk, put things off, waste time, or don't show gratitude for my wife's love) I start a vicious cycle of self-deprecation. I am fat; I am a procrastinator; I don't deserve Sam's love. These are all thoughts that adversely contradict self-love. These have been my thoughts and triggers for years and years. These are insecurities.

The biggest takeaway for me on all of this is that I KNOW if I can master the ability to truly love myself, I will be:

1. A better father,
2. A better husband, and
3. A better man.

I will be these things because I will no longer be telling myself behind the curtain that I'm a fraud, which I know affects my mood and my demeanor towards those around me in a negative way. In fact, I will remove the curtain and scrape away the veneer for good, because it no longer serves a purpose for me. That is my mantra. The outcome will be what I become. And no matter what, it will be enough.

Self-love requires you to engage more and more in

loving behaviors, eliminating the insecurities that make you question whether you are good enough and replacing the negative self-talk with messages of forgiveness and acceptance. Ask yourself, "Am I taking care of myself, nurturing myself and giving myself what I need to flourish and thrive?" Self-love means discovering what drives you and makes you sing, then doing that every day. It is not giving a shit about what anyone thinks. It is about just being you, being authentic. Self-love doesn't care what society's definitions are of your gender or race or how you should look or act. Self-love is taking care of you no matter what. It is stepping back with a sigh of satisfaction and bliss knowing that now you are ready to love everyone else.

Everyone is different when it comes to the specifics. You may even feel that self-love is a place where you already excel, and you don't need any more work on the subject. Awesome. I am not there yet, but endeavor to keep progressing. One of the tools I have used has been reproduced in a worksheet in the back of the book (The Self-Love Worksheet) that asks some tough questions and may help fast-track you to understanding the concept better.

CHAPTER 2

FROM IN LOVE TO TRULY LOVING

If you've never studied a new language, you should try it! Learning a different language is also learning a new way of looking at the world.

Depending on whom you ask there are as many as eight different words for types of love in ancient Greek. The more Paddy and I learn about these words, the more they make sense to us—much more so than the very confusing word "love." We use the same word to express a feeling we have for our parents as we do for our lovers, for our children and our country—not to mention food or cars or outfits. To feel each of these emotions, with all of their complexity, is to know they are not the same. And so the question begs: Can we truly understand love if the language we use to define it falls short?

Our eyes were further opened when we attended

a workshop with a highly regarded Peruvian Shaman who proclaimed very bluntly that we as humans know nothing about love. Jesus came to the earth to teach us about love, he explained, but we missed the message. And when you consider that the average person is likely to say "I love pizza" as readily as "I love you," the Shaman has a point. Given the current state of marriages and the world, we tend to agree with him. But we can change that.

To better understand love, we've got to expand our vocabulary. Learning the Greek names for love will give us the opportunity to explore its different types with more clarity, so let's define some of these in simplified terms[6] and then continue to use them throughout this book.

Eros: Sexual Passion

Named after the Greek god of fertility, Eros is the erotic, passionate, or sexual love you likely felt for your partner when you first met. This is the "madly in love" stage our society seems to be obsessed with. All "chick flicks" or romantic comedies are about this kind of love, the yearning, the fire, the keep-you-up-at-night, all-consuming love that takes hold of your entire being. It's the *Twilight* series, the Nicholas Sparks titles sprinkled across the best-seller list. Eros love is the love that possesses you.

---

6   *How Should We Live? Great Ideas from the Past for Everyday Life* by Roman Krznaric; *Colours of Love: An Exploration of the Ways of Loving* by John Alan Lee; *The Four Loves* by C.S. Lewis

Our society places an extraordinarily high value on Eros love. We want to get it, and then we expect those feelings to last. However, the Greeks did not hold this kind of love in such high regard. They viewed Eros as out of control, irrational, and dangerous like wildfire. We would add that Eros is like all extremes, unsustainable. If you continue to seek only this kind of love, you will always be searching for new partners with whom you can get back to this "high." Doing so comes at a cost, though. Chasing Eros will ultimately prevent you from experiencing the other types of deeper love with a life partner.

Philia: Friendship or Brotherly Love

Philia is the love you feel for very close friends or siblings. It is the love where you confide in people, where you share trust, where you have sacrificed for one another, and feel a sense of loyalty. The Greeks considered Philia one of the least natural loves because it isn't required for reproduction, but can you imagine your life or relationship without it? We choose this type of love as humans. We even name cities after it![7]

Storgē: Love Between Children and Parents

Storgē is familial love most exemplified by the love between children and parents. It is a love that happens naturally without effort and without regard to whether the object of that love is "worthy" of love. Storgē is love

---

7   Philadelphia, the City of Brotherly Love!

without discrimination. It is affectionate but not sexual. Storgē is a protective and caring kind of love revolving around a sense of commitment, loyalty, and trust.

Ludus: Playful Love

Ludus is a playful kind of love. Ludus is flirtatious and might include teasing and playing pranks on one another. You might go dancing, play sports together, enjoy the outdoors. This kind of love is more casual and frivolous than the others. It's no surprise then that Ludus is often described as activities of "young love."

Philautia: Self-Love

We will talk about self-love again and again and again in this book because we believe it is critical to happiness and building deep, loving relationships. There are however two kinds of self-love. There is narcissism, the type of self-obsession that cannot exist in healthy, loving relationships, and then there is the self-love that is caring about and taking responsibility for oneself. Guess which one we're here to talk about.

In our society, we're taught to put everyone else first. (We think this is particularly the case for women!) We're here to tell you, if you don't learn to take care of and love yourself, you risk burnout, physical and emotional health issues, resentment, feeling like a victim of your life, or even a martyr. And none of those will help or feed any of your relationships. We believe learning self-compassion is the only way you can have genuine and sincere compassion for others. We need to stop judging and being self-critical and extend ourselves compassion as well as forgiveness when we make mistakes.

It's amazing, we promise, but depending on your personality and how you were raised, self-love can be extremely difficult. The effort is worth it, however. As we discussed in the last chapter, once we learn to do this for ourselves, it becomes easier and natural to extend this same kind of love to everyone else.

Agape: Unconditional and All-Inclusive Love

Agape is described as selfless love, "God love," or charitable love. It loves without conditions, regardless of changing circumstances and it is one thing that appears in all world religions in some form or fashion. It described as love for everyone, gift love, or universal loving-kindness. We believe this is the love Jesus spent his time on earth trying to teach us. Agape is empathetic, patient, understanding, kind, faithful, forgiving and giving. It isn't critical. It doesn't judge. It recognizes that we are all connected. This love is conditional in only one respect: You cannot achieve it without loving yourself the same way.

And finally, we come to long-lasting love, the north star of your Love Endeavor:

Pragma: Truly Loving

Pragma is defined by some as "pragmatic love," meaning a practical love or love of convenience, and it could be used to describe the love that evolves from arranged marriages that never started with romantic love. We believe it is also the love you have to work for to evolve your partnership to the "true love" that will last your lifetime.

Pragma is about compromise, patience, intention, attention, intimacy, space, tolerance, and a whole slew of paradoxical thoughts, emotions, actions, and reactions. It is an elaborate and highly satisfying dance. We believe learning to love in Pragma and Agape love are the meaning of life—that is how amazing, uplifting, and transcendent these kinds of love can be!

Pragma's literal translation means "an action." And *action* is exactly what the entirety of this book is about. You have to take action to experience what we call Truly Loving. You have to endeavor to achieve it. Truly Loving is not some magical, elusive, exclusive emotion; it is something you earn by striving to have it.

All of the types of love are so interconnected that most modern languages lump them all into that one word— love. Even the modern Greeks don't regularly use all of these words for love. It is likely you can recognize aspects of each of them in many of your relationships.

Long-term friendships, for example, include Philia but usually also a little Ludus, and if you've been friends long enough, you will have granted some Agape love because your friendship would have to be strong enough to weather some storms.

In romantic relationships, as an example, many couples start out as friends—Philia. Friends often spend time together doing fun things like going out to eat, singing karaoke, or bowling—this would be playful, flirting Ludus. Things start heating up, and now there is also some physical attraction—moving into the sexual Eros type of love. One partner falls ill, and the other comes to their aid, taking care of them and nursing them back to health—this would be a time where it has shifted to Storgē love.

One partner makes a big mistake in the relationship—maybe they lie, have some indiscretion, or let their temper get the best of them at an inopportune moment—but the other partner continues to love them anyhow, granting them empathy, compassion, and forgiveness. This would require some level of Philautia because the forgiving partner would need to feel secure enough in their own skin to understand the actions of their partner are not a reflection of themselves. It would also be an act of Agape love in that the forgiving partner is required to reserve judgment and criticism in order to show empathy and compassion. Finally, this would also be one step on the road to Pragma because the forgiving partner has provided the space to their partner to make mistakes, providing the receiving partner a taste of unconditional love. It is a very comforting and secure feeling to know you are still lovable regardless of your mistakes and your shortcomings.

Even though there are aspects of each of these types of love in all of our relationships, each relationship will have a *primary* type of love, which can be helpful to identify.

HE SAID: THE MIGRATION AND WHY IT WON'T *ALWAYS* BE LIKE THIS

Being in love is awesome. There is a newfound need in your life that consumes all others. This need comes with a feeling of helplessness, gut-wrenching butterflies, and an ignorant bliss that makes it all feel so incredible. Most times being "in love" evolves into knowing you have found "The One." That knowledge then takes you to an even higher level of unique euphoria. It is an incredible feeling like no other you will have in your lifetime. Of course, there are still the rigors, responsibilities, and tasks of ordinary daily life, but they all seem secondary and somewhat superficial in comparison. When you are deep in Eros, it is everything.

Well, that's what it was like for me anyway. Some days, I felt reduced to nothing more than a grown man stumbling through life like a lovesick teenager. Why that analogy stopped at "teenager," I have not been able to figure out; "lovesick" always applied to me no matter what my age.

One must be careful not to get completely lost in love, however; it is easy sometimes to portray yourself as someone you are not while keeping her on a bit of a pedestal. You accept your partner for all her flaws in the beginning. You might even think some of them are cute and endearing. She can do no wrong! At the same time, you're trying to present yourself as flawless as possible. Some of your "quirks" may not be on display when you are around her, and some of your interests may be easily diverted. "No, I would much rather go with you to the still-life exhibition at the art gallery than watch football with my friends. Culture is important to me, and we can learn so much from the color palette of well-positioned fruit!"

Never mind the fact that you'll later make an excuse to step outside to fart unnoticed and call your buddies to bail on College Gameday. The truth is you love football and have no intention of replacing it with gallery strolls for the rest of your life.

Don't get me wrong, being in love is awesome and should not be diminished in any way. I am just pointing out that sometimes we become a bit less authentic, telling ourselves a story about how we may need to behave so as not to lose this "keeper" who has come into our life. This inauthenticity is simply a form of insecurity that is fueled by a fear of rejection. That fear cannot exist inside a person who loves himself. It is common, and I speak from experience. Both in my own behavior and that of people I have been in a relationship with. I am not perfect yet; I know you keep waiting for me to get there but it likely won't happen in this book.

So first things first, let's recognize we are being insecure and, after the third gallery stroll, get back to authenticity and casually mention that you prefer to watch college football on Saturday (and that it was you who crop-dusted the Van Gogh display.) Authenticity is sexy, and you shouldn't have an issue, but with all relationships there comes compromise. You will likely have some tradeoff with interests. The good news is that you will no longer be misrepresenting yourself as a non-gaseous art lover.

Another tendency, in the beginning, is to lose the ability to make a decision and mirror your happiness in theirs. "What do you want?" "That's what I want!" "You are so amazing," "It's like we're connected on so many levels." Romance is hidden around every corner, and you pull out all stops to make sure that you succeed in the love department.

We start out like the peacock during the mating ritual, our feathers and confidence are on full display as we strut to the front to win their affection. But once we win the prize, our feathers tuck back in and our stride becomes less flamboyant. And we have succumbed to the normality that sometimes can leave much of the romance in its wake. We stopped prioritizing the relationship as "What You Want, I Want" and slowly start diverting to "What I expect from You Is ..."

Sex is a great example of what I'm talking about here. Sex is usually not an issue in a new relationship; it is spectacular, new, and uninhibited. Gladly trying new things and intently focused on pleasing each other. Then later in the relationship, people tend to become more selfish, more inhibited, less willing and sometimes refusing to be playful altogether. Many, many couples end up in some variation of this. I won't say it is normal, just that it is not unusual. And to "bring back that loving feeling," we need to stop the pattern of thinking that chased it away.

"The Migration is in full swing or happened years ago, and we are stuck." So what now?

First off we need to remind ourselves: "I love this person." Ingrain that message in your brain and constantly be mindful of it. Only then can it translate into action. A good way to do that is to ask yourself: "Are my words and actions consistently loving?" and then modify accordingly.

For example, have you ever had to sit and listen to a couple say mean and nasty things to each other? Have you ever engaged in that behavior? Speaking like that to each other is not loving in any way. Would you ever have talked to each other like that at the beginning of your relationship? I will answer that with a resounding NO! So why would you do it now? Why say unloving things? The book *Crucial Conversations*[8] will say it is because we ourselves are hurt, and we will dive deeper into that idea later. The important thing is to recognize the behavior, catch yourself quickly, and remember to be loving instead. Being in love is easy. Being loving all the time takes work. It requires a different mindset, and you won't have the aid of the blind euphoria of new love.

---

8   Crucial Conversations is written by Kerry Patterson, Joseph Grenny, Ron McMillan, and Al Switzler

There are hacks to this, however. My friend Cassidy says "making out" with his wife of fourteen years keeps the romance high. He is obviously not in the beginning stages of Eros anymore, but he swears by it. I quietly thought "Well maybe that works for you, but ..." Then I looked it up and found an article by Elizabeth Weiss McGolerick[9] supporting Cassidy's claims. The article states that kissing stimulates secretion of oxytocin, which is a neuropeptide that, among other things, helps you feel trust, empathy, closeness, and increases sexual arousal. Whoa! So there you have it, Cassidy was right. It may not be new love euphoria, but it sounds pretty good to me and is certainly more sustainable.

I have another friend, Ryan, who is madly in love, and while he is not quite as lost as our non-gaseous art lover (as most people are not) he has made some adjustments to his routine that resulted in some negative self-talk. Ironically, this is the same friend who I spoke with for hours in Vietnam about self-love. He is as evolved as anyone on the concept but as vulnerable as the rest of us in practice. That is perfectly fine. No one reading this book, or any book for that matter, can claim perfection when it comes to self-love. Success is recognition and modification.

Back to Ryan.

"She has become my center of focus," he told me, "and

---

9   http://www.sheknows.com/parenting/articles/821684/love-hor-mones-natures-greatest-pain-relievers

I have let some of my routines slip considerably. She and our impending engagement have been the most important thing to me. Everything else seems to have fallen by the wayside."

"Dude," I said. "You see what you are doing, right?"

Then he said, "Well it's not that I am doing things I don't want to do. I am still happy."

I responded, "I get that, but you yourself told me that self-love sometimes requires triage. You recognize something's missing so take steps to do those certain things, the ones that you've put on the back burner, the ones that are gnawing at you right now and help you love yourself completely. Just correct it right now. It's that easy"

I recognize that in a new relationship what is the most important sometimes gets cloudy. And even if you are like Ryan and understand self-love, sometimes you can get sidetracked and not even notice. But when the love drug begins to wear off, you may start to harbor resentment. Remember, though, that it is ultimately your decision to prioritize the important pieces of your life and thus it's your responsibility to line them up accordingly in order of importance (triage).

I mentioned new love, mad love, euphoria and the love drug above. Let me explain what I mean. The reason we equate Eros to a drug is that being newly in love can have a similar impact on your brain. The euphoria you feel when in love is caused by endorphins and hormones—

most notably dopamine, the same hormone intensified by cocaine. When we are "madly in love" (Eros) we can become addicted to that high and strive to feel it always. When that happens, we may let other important things slip. These things happen; sometimes they are necessary, but we need to be mindful of the big picture and continue to take care of ourselves, to love ourselves.

Ryan was getting inconsistent with his regular exercise and meditation, usually morning rituals that helped him be much more balanced. By skipping those, he realized he was knocking his brain and body out of whack and getting down on himself for it. All I had to do was remind him that being the best version of himself was how he would bring his A-game to the relationship. By allowing the love drug to compromise that, he was creating a situation where he might start to build resentment when the euphoric high wears off. He realized immediately that by helping himself in this scenario he would strengthen the relationship over the long term, and that was all he wanted. He is a pretty smart dude.

I believe Sam and I exemplify Pragma love and we have come so much further than where we began. The butterflies are long gone, as is the ignorant bliss of being love struck. It took time, it took work, and it took compromise, but when you really love someone and choose to spend the rest of your life with them, it's worth it. That's why we are here. Now rather than just being in love, Sam and I have transitioned to Truly Loving. Truly loving someone means that you accept him or her for all that they are and focus on the best parts of that person.

Once you cross that bridge into Truly Loving, you open the door for a deep love that becomes an unbreakable bond and defines who you really are. However, you must first leap a hurdle: When the relationship transitions out of that euphoric, dopamine-fed state (Eros) to the long-term, long-lasting love that requires a lot more than feel-good brain chemicals to sustain it (Pragma). Truly Loving requires endeavor to flex, improve and grow. This chapter is about recognizing the difference between the Eros and Pragma and understanding that the migration has to happen from one to the next. The bulk of this book is how we describe our journey from Eros to Pragma.

SHE SAID: LOVE PARTNERSHIPS MUST EVOLVE OR THEY WILL DISSOLVE

When you fall madly in love, as Paddy mentions, chemicals are released in your brain that create a kind of natural high. This high, like all highs, can be very addicting. You feel good all the time! And who wouldn't want that feeling for the rest of their lives? And isn't that what the media would have you believe with the giant "Happily Ever After" at the end of a movie ending in marriage? Aren't you supposed to feel madly in love forever?

Honestly, I thought that. My guess is many people

believe this. I thought if I married the right person I would feel those drug-like highs forever. All of life would be easier in love, and there would be no such thing as temptation when I was madly in love. But in my marriage, just like all of my other relationships, Eros started to wane, and I wasn't feeling those drug-like highs of being madly in love as often or maybe at all. And like any junkie, I started trying to find it again. I wasn't just going to let those feelings go without a fight!

When we lived in Kansas City, we put some effort into rekindling those feelings together, and we had some success. We had some amazing date nights where sparks would fly! There were some others that were duds. However, there was a bit of desperation in trying to save Eros because I didn't know I couldn't have that all the time for the rest of my life. Just knowing that type of love isn't supposed to last would have been immensely helpful and might have made the transition out of Eros easier.

As things got tougher for Paddy and me, and I had all of that male attention at my job, I found myself seduced again by Eros as men flirted with and flattered me. I could get tastes of that Eros high guilt-free if nothing got physical. I think when I told Paddy we were done, I was hoping to be swept away by Eros with a new partner. When that didn't happen, I had the good fortune of being too busy to chase Eros. Had I persisted in chasing Eros, I would still be searching for the madly in love "Happily

Ever After" I dreamed about because doesn't exist. But worse, I would also never have had the opportunity to experience real love: Truly Loving.

You may still be saying to yourself; I can have that mad love Eros for the rest of my life! But I'm telling you, you cannot sustain true Eros as your primary love with your partner for a plethora of reasons. Eros is the spark that lights the fire and burns fast and hot. That white-hot flash cannot be the ultimate goal of your relationship, or you will fail. Your ultimate goal is for your love to evolve to Pragma and Agape. This is the perfect fire—it just may be what you came to this earth to do and learn, the meaning of life—and there is nothing more fulfilling or transcendental than this love.

Getting to this type of love and longevity in your partnership takes work. I'm not going to lie to you, the road between Eros and Pragma is long and arduous, but as I said, if you put in the work it will bring you more fulfillment than you ever knew was possible.

When we were first married, Paddy and I would often comment how we were the happiest couple we knew. We loved each other's company; we had lots of sex; we wanted to be together every moment—we were in Eros. However, our first year of marriage presented a number of challenges as we began the Great Migration from Eros to Pragma. It starts as soon as Eros begins to wane. You'll know when that happens by how you feel, and for some, it happens even before marriage.

When you start to feel yourself desperately trying to fan the dying flames or rekindle the embers of Eros, it's a good time to focus on some of those other kinds of love.

We believe working on fostering all of the types of love is time well spent. And a healthy, loving, long-lasting partnership will require skills in each of the types of love as your life unfolds. Now that Eros is waving goodbye, get comfy with the other types of love. (Don't panic, Eros will still occasionally show up in different phases of life with your partner. You just can't count on this kind of love—it's fickle.)

We talked all about **Philautia** (self-love) in the last chapter. This is crucial to start now no matter where you are in your relationship and you need to continue until you die and *especially* during the Great Migration from Eros to Pragma. Make sure you are taking care of yourself, and you'll bring your best self to any situation that presents itself.

Ludus is a great one to foster good, loving feelings towards one another. Play together! Paddy and I have a non-negotiable weekly date night. Sometimes we stay home and eat popcorn and watch movies. Sometimes we go out with friends on double-dates or to parties. Sometimes we go out, get drunk, and come home and have wild sex. We like to mix it up.

We also joke around A LOT. In case you didn't pick up on it yet, Paddy is hilarious. He plays little pranks on me, and if I can ever think of anything, I try to return the favor. He likes to lock me out of the car and pretend like he is unlocking the door so I jerk the handle ... for minutes at a time. If we're somewhere busy with lots of potential onlookers, he will also honk the horn and raise his hands up as if I'm unable to work a car door handle. He thinks this is hilarious and it makes everyone around us laugh—and I never mind being the butt of a joke. It's a fun time for me. No, really, I laugh as much as anyone. I think anything that brings laughter is a fun time, even if people are laughing at me. You'd think this kind of thing would get old. Maybe we're totally immature because we still laugh at this after twenty years.

Philia is another good one to start focusing on during the migration. All of the other couples we know who have lasted in their marriages also consider themselves to be best friends. They tell each other secrets, know exactly what's going on in each other's lives, share their feelings, hopes, desires, and dreams for the future! Friends build trust with one another over time by keeping confidences and showing up for each other. And your very best friends will believe in you even when you may not believe in yourself. Friends can hear the ugliest truths about you and still love and support you. If you have a best friend that isn't your partner, spend some time thinking about what makes that person your best friend. What have you done to build that friendship? Try doing those things with your partner.

Storgē is a tricky one with a partner because sometimes this love in action can sometimes make our partners feel like we are mothering or babying them but it is extremely useful and necessary once you understand it under certain circumstances.

The part of Storgē I'm referring to is the care you received as a child from your parents when you were sick or the love you received when you were emotionally distraught.

A few years ago Paddy injured his back. Paddy is a very proud and independent man who rarely gets sick or injured, and when he does, he usually refuses any help anyhow. But on this day he was in so much pain that he couldn't get out of bed. I called an ambulance and met him at the hospital. I stayed with him as they gave him some oral medications to ease the pain. They didn't seem to have much effect, and soon they wanted to run an IV. It was a teaching hospital, and they requested permission for a student to put in the IV. We agreed but after the fourth or fifth unsuccessful try, my mother lion came out, and I requested an experienced professional to come and properly insert the IV.

They gave him some drugs through the IV, but after hours of agony, he was still in pain. Again, my mother lion came out, and I demanded the doctor come in and do something more. They finally gave him something that worked, and he fell asleep.

This is the Storgē I'm talking about. I imagine

that, although we are not there yet, this loving, caring, and protective love will be extremely useful as we age and learn to take care of each other as our bodies and minds decline. Storgē is also the kind of love you tap into when there are traumatic events. We'll talk more about this in a later chapter, but know you are tapping into a special kind of love that you likely learned from your parents or other caregivers when you empathize, love, support, care for, and become protective of your partner. It has its time and its place and, if you don't pull it out when it's needed, the lack of Storgē love could also end your relationship.

Agape love is the kind you practice in your religion or your spiritual practices and can give you great comfort and a feeling of being grounded throughout your life and your love life. Focus on this bigger love can also help through this migration, especially if you practice it together with your partner.

Pragma is simply all of these kinds of love, used at the right times, over long periods of time. It is not merely a destination; it is the entire journey of your partnership. This whole book, as Paddy mentions, is a collection of techniques for making the migration from Eros to Pragma.

Eros love—the white-hot, fast-burning flame—can't, doesn't, and shouldn't last a lifetime. Pragma, the perfect fire, is sustainable, amazing, transcendent love well worth every bead of sweat you put into it.

So, put the things we discussed into practice. Work on developing those other types of love. We also have a worksheet in the back to assist you as you find yourselves in this transition (or perhaps you've already made it through but realize you didn't navigate it as well as you could have and need a little redo). This great migration is nothing to fear; it is another step forward in the path of a long-lasting Truly Loving relationship!

CHAPTER 3

EXPRESSING LOVE

Expressing love is critical. It is a crucial ingredient in every relationship. Do it well, and it can carry you through to Pragma; do it poorly, and you may not make it. Expressing love isn't as easy as it sounds. How, when and where we show love is often where we miss the boat. It is different for every couple, but most importantly it is different *within* the couple. Dr. Gary Chapman taught us there are five love languages we all fall into and helped define the how and why.

He also explains why we didn't figure out something so seemingly simple on our own. He explains (we are very loosely paraphrasing here) that when we have no point of reference, we usually stick to what we know. What we know is what we like. So when it comes to expressing love, most of us just fumble through it doing what we think feels right or good. It is usually recognized but often doesn't carry the same impact for the other person that it does for ourselves.

We believe that the path to Pragma is much shorter if you can express love in the most effective way your partner wants it most. What comes next is one of the best tools out there for learning ways to express love effectively.

THE 5 LOVE LANGUAGES

Without question, one of the most vital tools in our Love Endeavor is Dr. Gary Chapman's *The 5 Love Languages*. In fact, it has had such a hugely positive effect on our relationship that we had to dedicate part of our book to it! Needless to say, we consider it a MUST READ! In the book, Chapman asserts that everyone gives and receives love in different ways. Where couples can run into trouble, he says, is when they speak different love languages.

If you only speak Spanish and your partner only speaks Mandarin, you're going to have a tough time communicating, right? Well, the same goes with the love languages. It is possible (and probable) for one partner to be expressing love in a way that does not translate to the other partner as an expression of love. Dr. Chapman breaks these love languages into five different categories.

How many times have you bought a nice gift for your partner thinking it would put you over the top, only to get back a grateful indifference? Chances are you are not speaking your partner's primary love language. Once you and your partner understand each other's love languages, your expressions of love can become more deliberate and effective. You'll be better able to give and receive love in ways that resonate, which also means more happiness and fulfillment in your relationship!

Dr. Chapman offers an assessment on his website to determine your love language. If you haven't read the book yet, we suggest you go take the assessment RIGHT NOW before you read any further (and maybe try to convince your partner to take it too):

www.5lovelanguages.com

HE SAID: WHAT HAVE YOU DONE FOR ME LATELY?

You will note throughout this book that household chores are a big deal for Sam when I don't help. When I do? Wow. It always blows my mind how she can get so excited by me doing a load of laundry. I could build an addition on the house, and it won't turn her on as much as me straightening up and doing some dishes.

Understanding this did not happen until I read *The 5 Love Languages* with Sam. It was a huge aha moment for me that explained so much. Praising her efforts also goes a long way. If she is doing the work, I make sure to show gratitude—and then try to remember to do it next time! (Helpful Tip: Use this opportunity to introduce some

Ludus. To attract attention to my efforts I have cleaned in nothing but a skimpy apron before. She noticed a lot sooner, and when I was done, we moved from her love language straight to mine. *I just wish she had not posted the pics of me cleaning on her Instagram!*)

SHE SAID: BUT I TOUCHED YOU JUST LAST WEEK

Touching and being touched is another love language Dr. Chapman describes. This love language is Paddy's primary, and we have yet to encounter a relationship where one of the partners doesn't have this as their primary love language, although I'm sure they are out there. When we made changes in this area of our relationship, the results were immediate, and we believe it is so important we gave touching its own chapter: Better Sex (and More of It!).

SHE SAID: LOVE LANGUAGE MISFIRE

Personally, I don't get too excited about getting gifts, nor do I spend much time, energy, or money giving gifts to anyone. So I rarely think about *giving* gifts out of the blue.

It was a point of contention in our household during our first ten years of marriage. While I was traveling, Paddy would wonder what I got him when I came back. It was usually nothing. However, on one flight home I remembered him complaining about how I never brought him any presents and, as luck would have it, the duty-free cart came through right then. So I bought him a watch. He LOVED that watch so much—or at least he did until he was on an international flight and saw it on the duty-free cart. Then he HATED it because it didn't represent my thinking of him while I was gone; it stood for my remembering I *should* buy him a gift only when I was on my way home. Fail.

HE SAID: IT'S NOT ABOUT THE GIFT

As to Sam's story above, it was during the first ten years that this was an issue and I recognized later that my need to get a gift from her after she had been traveling was likely more seeded in insecurity. "You didn't think about me while you were gone? Waaaaaahhh." I don't know how important gifts are for me anymore; it's kind of a non-issue. I think now I would much prefer to give gifts than get them. Unless it's whiskey, I like it when people give me good whiskey.

SHE SAID: I'M SO GLAD HE'S OVER IT

Paddy always wanted gifts, but it was hard to shop for him because he'd always buy anything he wanted. And then if I did happen to find something to buy him there was always an inquisition about how much I paid for it, which always made me feel like whether I got a good deal on something trumped the gift itself. We rarely exchange gifts anymore, and I couldn't be happier about it.

Time and Priorities

Three out of the five love languages require you spend time with your partner and the other two could happen while you are spending time with your partner also but it's not mandatory.

Here's the thing: if you don't carve out time with your partner, your relationship will decay. The major issue that caused my break-up with Paddy, as I have mentioned, was prioritizing my job. Said in another way, I did not prioritize my relationship with Paddy. By not prioritizing our relationship, we had very, very little time together at all with my travel schedule and none of it was spent working on our relationship. When I was home spending time with him, I was always at my rope's end, was never intentional, and had zero tools to make things better. We may have been spending time together, but it wasn't time spent expressing love to each other in ways we understood.

Eros was gone and, on some level, I knew we should be going on dates (playing in Ludus) and spending time talking (developing Philia), but because I wasn't prioritizing our relationship, I was too tired to be bothered with any of that. When we were together, we spent some time with friends, but when we were alone, we watched movies or TV. Or, more accurately, I slept while Paddy watched movies and TV.

This lack of time combined with an ignorance of how we should be spending the small amounts of time we did have together led to such a degradation of our relationship that I didn't really want to spend any time together.

If your relationship is important (and my guess is that it is if you are bothering to read this book) you need to prioritize your partner and spending time with them—developing Ludus and Philia and expressing love to one another by speaking each other's love languages. Plan it and put it in your calendars each week and treat it as a sacred, non-negotiable commitment.

When our kids were young, Paddy and I tried hard to have one date night a week. We were broke, and some date nights consisted of little more than dropping the kids off at the in-laws and driving back to our house to hang out together. Your time together may or may not include sex (though it should—skip to next chapter for more on that) but try to be fully present and listen to one another, even if it's just during the drive to and from the movie theater together. There are few things as gratifying as knowing someone has heard and understood you. It helps you connect with each other on that intellectual and potentially emotional level—all good things to build intimacy.

Spend some of your time together having fun! You might've heard that couples or families that play together stay together. We think it's true.

Maybe try new things outside your comfort zone. There is nothing like a little healthy fear to bring a couple together. I'm not kidding. Paddy and I recently went on a trip to Cabo, and there is a place there with zip lining, bungee jumping, and a giant swing. The swing allows two people to drop from three hundred feet above a beautiful desert canyon and then swing in a pendulum of a two-hundred-and-forty-foot radius at over eighty mph. I was petrified, and I think Paddy was a little freaked out too. But we went out there and did it together. Something about that experience bonded us that day, and the high lasted many weeks as we retold the story and watched the video. It was Ludus love in action!

Don't forget about carving out time for yourself either. Prioritizing time and space just for you is part of Philautia. *The Miracle Morning* by Hal Elrod is an excellent way to start your day by investing in yourself. Paddy and I both get up early to go through our morning routines before we start our days. You need to make a habit of taking care of yourself in order to best serve your relationships. Show yourself a little love first, and then expressing love to others becomes more effortless.

HE SAID: THAT'S EASY FOR YOU TO SAY, OUR SITUATION IS DIFFERENT...

Most of you with young kids are trying to understand how you are supposed to find all of this extra time to give yourself and your significant other. I get it; there is none. You are on the go from dawn till dinner and then some.

School, after school activities, breakfast, dinner ... shit, we forgot to pack their lunches! Use your lunch break to drive to the school and hand out meal money. I feel like I need a nap after just writing that.

We are all busy. And some calendars are fuller than others when it comes to squeezing in all this additional self and love endeavor. But if we remember that we are here to improve and grow and become the best lover we can be to ourselves and partners, we must make room. It doesn't need to be a significant chunk of time. Just enough to express your love. With small kids, you have to pick and choose your windows. Sam and I had kids right out of the chute while we were still deep in Eros. We would sometimes only have three to five minutes to be romantic or playful before one of the kids rolled up crying with a load in their pants. You have to take those minutes wherever you can get them.

As you get more settled into your relationship, it becomes easier to "not have time." I get it; you are a slave to your schedules and the schedules of your kids. There is little room, and you are too tired or don't feel like it. I can only say this one way. Make time. If your relationship is not where you want it to be then, you must make time.

I have heard said that one of the best things you can do for your kids is to show them how much you love their mom or dad. That has always made sense to me and dovetails right into the theme of this book. It is also an incredible teaching opportunity for your kids. Where else are they going to learn what love looks like if not from you? It sure as shit isn't Hollywood. It is up to you to show them, and there is no better way to do that than to consistently show love to yourself and your partner the best way you can.

Manage your self-talk to enable success.

Sam mentioned *The Miracle Morning* by Hal Elrod. This book, along with *The Magic of Believing* by Claude M. Bristol, and *Think and Grow Rich* by Napoleon Hill are all three awesome books that discuss the power of positive affirmations.

An affirmation is something you tell yourself repeatedly and intentionally to convince your mind that you have it, or are it. The power of affirmation has been proven over and over again by people from all walks of life. They all share the common theme that if you have the discipline, you can change or improve many things about yourself by making daily affirmations and visualizing. If you want to dive much deeper into this topic, then I suggest starting with one of the books above. They are all great, and you will get life-changing knowledge from them.

The reason I mention affirmations is that they are very, very powerful and are always at work in our lives whether we practice them daily or don't even know what they are. Most affirmations, unfortunately, show up in the form of negative self-talk. One of the most common

I see on a daily basis is "I am terrible with names." Yes, you are, and you always will be as long you tell your brain that every time you have a chance to remember a name.

Your subconscious mind is where almost ALL of your brainpower exists. We have all heard we only use ten percent of our brain, right? Well, that is not accurate, we USE one hundred percent of our brain. Science, however, can only explain HOW we use ten percent of it. Glial cells (the other ninety percent of the brain) control things like affirmations, habits, and routines, and we are tapping into that every minute without realizing it. It is where our habits and beliefs are stored that dictate our self-talk.

Have you ever spouted out an answer to a question when you have no idea how you knew that? Have you ever had a feeling about a number and knew it was the answer to an equation only never to duplicate that ability again? For example, I believe I can usually get close to a grocery bill or a restaurant bill by blurting out the first number that comes to mind. And it works for me all the time. I would even say that the times I am most wrong is when I think about it too long.

Science has trouble backing this stuff up because they still can't explain it. Therefore you can go find as much to refute the power of affirmations as you can to acknowledge them in the science community. But in the *success community,* you will have an incredibly tough time finding anyone who tells you this stuff doesn't work.

So it's just a matter of who you want to be. You still with me? Good. You want to succeed? Great choice!

So what does this have to do with your relationship?
How we talk to ourselves, the mantras we repeat between our ears, can either help us to succeed faster or hinder our growth. It is no different in your relationship. How you talk about your partner out loud and what you say to yourself about them will directly influence your ability to be loving. If I am thinking to myself or saying out loud how sexy, smart and beautiful Sam is, I almost immediately want to be with her, hold her, tell her those things and show her my gratitude. However, there is an adverse thought process that exists all too frequently in relationships and makes expressing love more difficult.

I know so many people in my community, as well as my tribes who do daily affirmations to help improve and manifest the things they want for themselves and their futures—and it is awesome to see the good things that come from their work! BUT I know many of the same people who have also built up a huge amount of negative affirmations toward their spouse or partner. Here are some I have heard in the last few years:

> *"I just don't have the same passion for her as I used to for someone else." "No matter what I do I can't figure out women, especially my wife." "I would love to be single again," "I just hate her."*

I know the last one was harsh, and when I peeled back a few layers, the man who said it admitted he doesn't hate his wife; he still loves her, but "hate" was the word he was saying to himself. Think about how powerful that self-talk could be.

Typically, your spouse is a major element of your *Why*. It doesn't matter how much money you make if that person, your best friend and the one you chose to spend the rest of your life with, is unhappy and doesn't get priority. If that is the case, let's take a minute and think about what kinds of things we say to ourselves and about our partners. Are you reinforcing negative messages toward your spouse or relationship? Time to change that head noise and maybe even add a positive affirmation or two to your daily routine.

SHE SAID: YOUR *WHY*

Paddy and I talk quite a bit about our *Why* since we've been back together, meaning we look not only at *what* we are doing but *why* are we doing it. I very much lost sight of my *Why* as I let my job become my entire life before our break-up. I also know the things I was saying in my head and sometimes out loud about Paddy were not flattering. Perhaps had I changed my head, I could have pulled it out of my ass faster.

BACK TO HE SAID:

If you are not an "affirmations person," begin by

recognizing the negating language you use and change it. If you say, "My relationship sucks" all the time, it will eventually be true. Conversely, if you say, "I am striving to have an incredible relationship, and I will do everything I can to improve and maximize it," then you're creating a very different reality. If you start here and implement the other things we are talking about, before long, you will be able to say: "We have an incredible relationship!" "My partner is amazing!" "I am excited to see her/him." If this is the soundtrack between your ears, then you are in a much better place to express love than you are if you are constantly reinforcing the negative. It is so much easier to express love when we think lovingly.

CHAPTER 4

BETTER SEX (AND MORE OF IT!)

Seeing as how this is a book about romantic relationships, we would be remiss to exclude a discussion of sex. Plus, we have a lot to say about it!

Have you ever brought up romantic relationship issues with a therapist? One of the first things they seem to ask is about your sex life. We're not therapists but it seems like asking how a couple's sex life is going is like taking the temperature of the relationship—it's not going to tell you what the problem is but it will be a relatively accurate indicator of whether the relationship is healthy or not.

If you follow our words of advice in this chapter, you will have more sex and the sex will be better. We know, big promise but read on.

SHE SAID: JUST SAY YES!

As he never fails to mention, Paddy is a touch guy. And

although cuddling and hand-holding and tickling his back are all nice, if I don't go in for some sexual touch at least a couple times a week, the wheels start to come off our love bus.

Me? I grew up in a household with very little snuggling or touching. Neither my sister or I like to be touched very much—there is a bubble you should enter only at your own risk—so I feel like it must have been something we were raised with (or maybe some genetic defect?). In any case, touch is not my thing. Don't get me wrong, I love a good massage and a roll in the hay, but I can go months without either one.

Needless to say, our sex life was always this weird point of contention for Paddy and me. After I found out that it was Paddy's love language, I realized that when we made love, he felt the wave of love and appreciation I felt when he mopped the floor. It all made sense! So, I tried to do a better job, or so I thought, of speaking his love language. The minimum was once a week-ish—unless I had a headache or my period, or my stomach wasn't right, or any other myriad excuses I could come up with to get out of it. (Not unlike all of the excuses Paddy would have for not mopping the floor.)

Then one day we were discussing our sex life—again— and he asked me, "Have we ever had sex, and you regretted it?" I thought, and thought, and thought, and told him very honestly: Never. Even if I didn't have an orgasm or the kids caught us in the act, or even the time

I got those horrible rug burns on my knees, I couldn't recall one time in our lives when I regretted having sex with him. So we agreed to conduct a little experiment: I would say yes every time Paddy wanted to have sex for a month. We called it "Just Say Yes."

I prepared myself for the sex-o-rama that I imagined (feared) was about to befall me. We did make love a few times those first couple days, but after that, I realized how subtle his sexual advances had become... I was having a hard time knowing if I was supposed to Just Say Yes! When Paddy made a subtle advance, and I asked him if this was a Just Say Yes moment, he would timidly ask, "Do you want it to be?"

What was going on here?

I'll tell you what was happening. I had rejected Paddy so many times that he was afraid to initiate sex, even with our agreement. No one wants to feel rejected or unwanted or unloved, and I realized that every time I ignored or rejected his attempts at intimacy, Paddy felt those negative feelings. It was heartbreaking to realize that I had caused him to feel that way! I decided I would begin initiating during our experiment. Interestingly enough, I think just making the decision to initiate sex made me feel more sexual, sexier—and it grew Paddy's confidence also.

And after the month of our experiment...we never stopped! Some magical things happened during that month, and we weren't about to call it off. Now the deal is if either of us initiates, we Just Say Yes!

It took me a good deal of self-reflection to figure out why I'd been so resistant to having a lot more sex. First of all, as I mentioned, I love a roll in the hay. I love having sex with Paddy. Looking back, I feel like I resisted his sexual advances because I viewed it as some "wifely duty."

Well, that and I had this perception of myself that I'm going to share with you now in all of my vulnerability. No holds barred. Because I think there are other women who can and will relate.

I was taught that you never had sex with someone unless you loved each other and felt a strong emotional and intellectual connection. That connection was far more important than the sex. That anyone who tries to pressure you into having sex should be arrested. And while those teachings probably served me well when I was young, they made marriage a little confusing.

Here was a man who was *always* trying to pressure me into having sex. And it didn't matter if I felt any emotional or any other connection with him. Often sex was the very last thing on my mind when I felt exhausted, frustrated, disappointed, or otherwise uninterested in Paddy, and it always seemed to be the first thing on his mind. I felt, well, *insulted* that he would treat me like a SLUT.

No one told me the rules change when you're in a committed relationship!

I had a good friend when we lived in Kansas City, Gabby, who was happily married to a man who was practically the one hundred percent opposite of her. She was loud, funny, and you could describe her personality as bigger than life! She was always the life of the party. And her husband, Ron, was quiet—so quiet it was hard to get to know him. He was a little anti-social and didn't always attend our gatherings. Outside of them both being extremely intelligent, they were opposites in every way.

It was nearly impossible for Paddy and me to fathom how they could stay married, let alone how they could be so happy with each other. So one day I asked her, "What is the secret to your happy marriage?"

She looked me right in the eyes and without blinking or hesitating she said, "Sex. And lots of it."

I was floored! I never forgot what she said but, unfortunately, it took me a long time to implement her advice. The month we started Just Say Yes, Paddy and I both immediately relaxed. Sex wasn't anything that needed to be discussed; there were no decisions to make, no negotiations necessary; it was easy. We just do it. (Oh, and let's not confuse "do it" with actual sex. We don't always have intercourse, but Just Say Yes always ends with someone—hopefully both of us—having an orgasm.) There is no fear for either of us of feeling rejected, unwanted, or unloved.

The other thing that happened was Paddy got really happy! He still walks around like the cock of the walk because he gets laid anytime he wants. AND, he is more loving, open, and willing to speak my love language. It intensified our sense of intimacy ten-fold.

But mostly, I changed.

I changed my perception of sex, my sexuality, and myself. I realized I didn't need to "be in the mood" to have sex. I didn't need to feel passionate, or emotionally or intellectually connected at the moment for sex to be enjoyable with Paddy—often sex is the catalyst that helps me feel more loving and connected to him. I started to see it as a beautiful, enjoyable physical experience I choose to have with my partner no matter what the circumstances are.

Sex has become the way I am able to show my unconditional love for Paddy—a clear display of Pragma and Agape love, a physical way to tell him that I will love him no matter what is going on in and around our world. There is a kind of transcendence that must happen for you to engage in this intimate act when you are experiencing negative emotions towards one another. You have to step out of your ego, the part of you that is interested only in protecting yourself, the part that manifests fear, anxiety, distrust, and anger.

Then you must step into your higher self, the part of you that knows you must take risks to find true happiness and that you get what you give. Your higher self knows love is the meaning of life and drives you to give it every fiber of your being! When we can step out of our ego for the sake of our love, the experience softens both of us and gives us immediate, greater perspective. It is much easier to talk after sex than in the throes of an argument.

(I also started wanting it more. Go figure—I am hitting my sexual prime! Too bad I missed Paddy's sexual prime by like thirty years...)

Sex is also something I share with ONLY Paddy. I know there are lots of different partnerships and ways sex lives work. We have zero judgment as we've experimented with some of that, but in our partnership, we've decided sex is something we reserve for only each other. That in and of itself makes it a sacred act for us.

But what if ...

When I suggested Just Say Yes to a friend recently as a first step in healing her relationship, her response was, "How am I supposed to do that when I feel so much resentment towards him?" She proceeded to list all of the things her husband hadn't done for her lately amongst some other things he had done she didn't care for.

So how do you get beyond the resentment to engage in this intimate act?

You choose to.

Firstly, recognize that when you need to heal a relationship you have to start somewhere, and someone has to start. Someone has to make the first move to bring the love back into the relationship. Sex is such a clear and simple way to bring the love back, especially when your partner is a touch person.

Secondly, do not be fooled into believing all of your

emotions deserve of your attention and merit action. If you do, it allows your emotions to drag you around your life. You may not be able to decide how you feel—this is something that just happens in our minds and our bodies fueled by the thoughts we have—but you can choose how you act (or don't act) on those emotions.

When I have a negative emotion, I first allow myself to feel it fully. If you deny the feeling or try to change it too quickly, it will come back. I focus on how the negative emotion feels in my body: Where do I feel it? What does it feel like there? Does it burn or tingle or poke? I let my body go through all of the physicality of the emotion. I cry if my body wants to cry, with a lump in my throat and tears streaming down my face, or I experience the wave of adrenaline rushing through me if I feel angry. I observe myself in the emotion with as little judgment and as much compassion as I can bring to it. And then I ask myself what this emotion might be trying to tell me without allowing my thoughts to tangle me down into the details of the current scenario.

Let's use resentment as our example. First, I check in physically. For me, resentment feels hot like anger; it feels icky in my stomach. I then observe my emotions. Resentment tells me I feel hurt and in pain. It is fueled by thoughts of being treated poorly or unfairly. I know that when I feel resentful, I'm making assumptions. I assume my partner has treated me this way both knowingly and intentionally. Or I unfairly believe my partner should already know their action or inaction would be hurtful to me.

I recognize that feeling resentful is self-absorbed. That I'm only taking my feelings into consideration. That I'm blaming Paddy unfairly or ignoring things I may have contributed to the situation or cycle. Now I need to decide if I will take action and, if I do, what action I will take. It may surprise you to know that, when it comes to resentment, I've figured out that the best immediate action to take is...nothing.

Through—ahem—"trial and error," I've learned that I should not take any action while I'm in the middle of feeling this (or any) negative emotion. I know that I might not be able to act with as much control as I will need to get the results I want. The best move I can make is to take a time-out.

Next I think, "What do I want?" In the case of my close relationship, I likely want my partner to change, so I no longer feel resentful. If he's the one making ME feel bad, he should be the one to change, right? This is the big mistake most people make while they are trying to "fix" their relationships. Since you have zero control over whether your partner changes or not, you need to focus on something realistic you CAN do.

You can start.

You can be the one to take the first steps towards healing your relationship.

And one of the quickest and easiest ways to make

that first move is to begin speaking your partner's love language.

So again, we're sort of back where we started. You know you are supposed to start speaking your partner's love language, and you have felt your resentment fully in all of its discomfort, sooooo now what?

Gratitude. Practice some gratitude.

It is possible to give your positive emotions a much-needed boost, and one of the best ways to do it is to practice gratitude. We devote a full chapter to gratitude and forgiveness later in this book because your ability to practice these emotions will determine your ability to love your partner as deeply and wholly as possible.

Personally, I like to see my gratitude sitting right in front of me. There's something about seeing the words that makes them easier for me to internalize. Give it a try and see for yourself! Get out a piece of paper and write a full page of things you love about your partner and the things you feel grateful for in them. Here is what mine looks like:

> *I love Paddy's chameleon eyes that change colors with the colors of his shirt. I love his bright smile, his hairy chest, and his gray hairs. I love how gracefully he is aging. I love his laugh and his sense of humor. I love the way his sense of humor pushes the envelope of "appropriate" and can immediately disarm people with*

laughter. I love watching people laugh and feel joy from Paddy's jokes and comments. I love Paddy's huge heart, his desire to help any and everyone. I love his love for dogs. I love how Paddy works hard and willingly to support our goals and dreams. I love how Paddy plans all of our vacations. I love how Paddy never complains about how dirty our house gets. I love how Paddy's eyebrow could shelter us in a storm.

If you're still struggling with this activity, try thinking back to when you first met and fell in love; the things that you loved about your partner then probably still hold true today, even if you haven't seen them surface in a while. And if you are still at a loss, put the paper in your pocket and during the next few days make it your MISSION to find things to be grateful to your partner for. Don't give up—you can ALWAYS find gratitude.

Practice this exercise enough, and you will feel more loving towards your partner. THEN strike while the iron is hot! Go get 'em now and make the deal. Just Say Yes!

If you don't like sex, you need to read a different book. If you haven't figured out what you like sexually, that is a different quest entirely but one worth pursuing!

I challenge you: Try Just Say Yes to sex for a month and see what happens. I bet it will change your lives.

HE SAID: DON'T FUCK THIS UP!

My subtitle above is a bit of a joke, but in truth it was probably something I thought after a week or so of Just Say Yes. How cool would that be? You can have sex whenever you want! If I can get word of this chapter out, men or those who are more physical will be the ones bringing this book home. "Honey, let's read this book about strengthening our relationships together. I heard the best way to read it is to skip around, so let's start with chapter ... oh, I don't know chapter four maybe?"

That would be one way to fuck this up, so I don't recommend it. But hey, this is a short book so tough it out, it's worth it!

In the first week, Just Say Yes was a bit of a test for me to see if Sam would come through on what she promised. I threw it out there two or three times a day, so I could understand what the real boundaries were. I was able to get her to say no on the second day when asked her in the produce section of the grocery store. She passed with flying colors because even if she had said yes in the grocery store, I would not have followed through.

Historically, I typically tried for sex five or six times a week and got it maybe one. I think sex for a lot of people who have been together for a while is like that. You get into routines and habits that start defining where, when, and how you have sex. Many times you start to tell yourself a story about how sex needs to be good to be worthy of your time.

That's where Sam was. She was a morning person and was in the habit of giving me a window between seven thirty and eight thirty a.m. right after her shower. That was about the time my phone would start blowing up with emails and work-related things, and my stress level was rising. So I was not always in a position to accommodate.

I was a night person. I like to go to bed and fool around. She was always "too exhausted" and would say, "Let's do it in the morning." Sometimes I could trick her by saying, "You go ahead and go to sleep. I am just going to go down on you for a little while." If I got that far I could always change her mind and it was great. That is what prompted the question. "Have you ever said yes and then regretted it?"

The funny thing is that after Just Say Yes was in full swing and Sam had passed the initial test, I kind of backed off on asking for sex. Before, I felt like I needed to ask daily in order to find common ground weekly. Now, since she has agreed to say yes, I might only ask two or three times a week, and I try to be conscientious of how she is feeling.

We also seem to be going through a bit of a shift— maybe it's due to her sexuality, or maybe it's due to more frequent sex, but sometimes she will ask or initiate more than I do. All I can say about that is: Awesome!

How to Find Passion (It's right where you put it)
I had my first epiphany about two and half years into

our marriage. Sam and I were in an intimate moment, and I remember thinking, "Man, there just isn't much passion here. It feels like she is just going through the motions. I don't know if I can handle having sex with the same person for the rest of my life if it is going to be this passionless." These were my thoughts during and as we lay there afterward.

Then it hit me. What was I bringing to the table just then? Wasn't I just going through the motions as well? I was providing zero passion from my side, so why would I expect any in return? I decided then that I would not be someone who expected something like passion from someone else. I would BE passionate and see where it got me.

The next time we were intimate, I started being more in the moment and hyper-focused on everything good about that moment as well as focusing on Sam and what she was feeling in that moment. It is true. When you give, you get back more than you ever expected. Our sex life has been fantastic ever since I had that realization and decided to change.

I have had to remember this passion epiphany a few more times in my life outside the bedroom. Times when I felt burnt out with my business or felt like I was not getting enough out of groups I was involved in. Each time when I stepped outside myself and asked: "What am I giving?" My answer was always "not much." I was giving nothing and expecting everything. Try as I may, I have to keep remembering that has never worked for me.

Now, once I recognize it, I immediately choose to turn the tables on the situation. I double-down and re-apply myself. I focus on the now and what can I do to make it better. I put my attention on the good things I may have lost sight of at the moment. Then I decide to make more of a contribution. Smile, and then add as much value as I can muster, I find passion every time. Do you know why? It was never lost in the first place! It's always there just waiting to be applied. Passion is where you place it, plain and simple.

Now that you know the secret of finding passion, go apply your efforts to the things that need it most. Then sit back and watch how fulfilling those things become. Sounds too easy, doesn't it? I promise it works. Just be the giver, and you will receive.

Train Your Lover

I thought I would throw this in since we are talking about getting lucky. During Eros, we are turned on by everything. The newness can usually carry us for a while. But as we migrate to Pragma and get more into routines and let our inhibitions grow, sex can become just okay. I know plenty of couples who have echoed this sentiment. My advice? Don't let that happen!

If I were the same lover Sam had married, no way would we still be together. Fortunately, she trained me well by communicating a lot about what she likes and what she doesn't like. "Move up," "More to the left,"

"More gentle," "Yeah, that's it." She trained me so well that I think it was a significant factor in saving our marriage. Even though we were split up, she allowed me to seduce her throughout the separation. I figured it was my subtle game that reeled her back in, only later to find out that she just wanted sex with someone who she knew did it right.

If you find sex becoming less than spectacular, then one or both of you are not communicating enough. Or possibly you have narrowed your routine so much that it is becoming boring. Don't forget about Ludus! It has its place in the bedroom as much as anywhere. Be playful, stretch out the foreplay, reevaluate your inhibitions and expand your horizons some. Educate yourselves on new things to try, and then try them out. Especially you parents. Sometimes we change physically and need to go about it in different ways. Communicate how you are feeling, what feels good and what doesn't. Do whatever it takes to get back to having great sex again.

SHE SAID: STRANGE POSITIONS, RANDOM PLACES, TOYS, AND PORN

I don't think it's necessary to go into detail on any of these. I'll leave it to your imagination, and that is exactly the point. I would encourage you all to open your minds to new sex stuff with your partner. Some of my most memorable and pleasurable sexual experiences involved one or more of the things in the subtitle. I always thought those things were nasty and dirty, but now I think that they can be fun!

CHAPTER 5

THE CONSTANT STRUGGLE FOR THE SAME PAGE

Once you have committed to a partner and you're in a serious relationship, there are decisions you used to make on your own that you now have to share with your partner. This is especially true if you have children and/or cohabitate. Sure, there are plenty of decisions you will still make independently—but when you decide to share your life with someone else, it also means designing your life and making decisions together.

There are two places where finding the same page is critical: First, you need to determine which decisions need to be made together. Once you know which decisions you will share, the next step is to find that same page so you can come to an agreement. And to do that, it is all about communication!

SHE SAID: OPPOSITES ATTRACT AND THEN DISAGREE ON *EVERYTHING*

I can't tell you what percentage of couples are opposites of one another. Paddy and I are opposites in many, many ways. I am a neat freak, and he is not. I say work hard; he says work smart. I am an introvert who is slightly risk-averse; Paddy is an extrovert who is very comfortable taking risks. I could go on and on here.

I think part of why people are often attracted to their opposites is because we subconsciously recognize those things that will make us more complete, to fill in the holes so to speak. And this can be an amazing thing when it works smoothly. However, it also can be a fairly consistent source of misunderstandings, discomfort, disagreements, and flat-out fights. Forever.

So how do you navigate those differences?

Communication, communication, communication! And MOST of the communicating I'm talking about is actually listening. Fully focused, not just on the words your partner is speaking but also their tone, body language, and facial expressions. Trying to understand him or her. Intently and actively listening.

I hate to break it to you, but multi-tasking while you "listen" doesn't count.

I always thought I was paying attention when Paddy was talking, but I counted those times when I was looking at shit on my phone—playing games like Trivia Crack and Words With Friends or cruising Facebook, and responding to Paddy with a head nod or a "yeah"—as listening. I mean I *could* hear him after all.

That's how I ended up agreeing to go on a trip to hang out with his rugby buddies in Butt Fuck, West Virginia. Clearly, I wasn't paying as much attention as I thought I had been. Spending my vacation traveling fourteen hours to a dingy old hotel to hang out with a bunch of glory-days-reliving dudes was the wake-up call I needed to make a change in my listening habits.

HE SAID: FROSTBURG

Okay, first of all, we were in Western Maryland, not Butt-Fuck, West Virginia. And they were not "rugby" buddies; it was a lacrosse team reunion. Oh, and that shitty hotel was the nicest one in town. Bam! Same page. That was easy.

Actually, it makes no difference to me whether the event was in Maryland or West Virginia, or whether it was rugby or lacrosse—what matters is that Sam agreed to come along and share it with me because I asked her to. How we got to that page is of little importance. How she remembers it doesn't matter either. She went, and I love her for it. End of story.

BACK TO SHE SAID:

Changing my habit was a bit harder than I expected. It was easy to give Paddy my full attention when he was talking about something that interested me, but what about those times when it wasn't? What about those times where his interest or viewpoint is the opposite of mine? I had to work out a solution that made it easier to up my attentiveness during those times when my mind started to wander. The trick I've learned is to tap back into my gratitude for him.

For instance, Paddy loves—insists on, actually—getting a good deal. Sometimes he brings home things we don't need, but he couldn't pass up the deal. I rarely buy things we don't need, but I when I do, I buy them without too much thought about if I'm getting the most for my money. But I've found things to appreciate about my deal-hunting husband.

NOW, when he goes on and on about a great deal he found, I think about how very appreciative I am that he works hard to find them. We'd be tens of thousands of dollars poorer if I were in charge of the majority of our shopping and travel! Plus, I recognize how much joy he gets out of the accomplishment, and I love it when he is happy! So I set the intention to listen, find things to appreciate and work very hard to give him my full attention. Paddy deserves nothing less.

Here are some more tips for improving your listening skills:

Remove all distractions. Stop whatever you're doing, and focus on what your spouse is saying so much that you could repeat what they said back to them.

Some communication experts say you should then also **repeat back what you heard**. I would love this, but Paddy does not have the patience for this kind of communication. If I repeat what he said back to him, he'll respond with, "I just said that."

Instead, my policy has been that if the conversation is about something important or I'm in any way confused about what is being discussed, then the repeat-back is a great strategy. It not only shows the other person you are listening if the topic is important, but it also prevents miscommunication because it gives your partner the opportunity to clarify the message, just in case it wasn't received correctly.

The repeat-back strategy is also extremely helpful when the conversation becomes emotional, if the other person seems agitated or annoyed in any way, or if you begin to feel upset or irritated. According to the research conducted by the authors of *Crucial Conversations*, when a conversation starts to get emotional, most people go into Fight or Flight mode. They either stop listening because they are thinking about what they are going to say next, how they will launch their defense or counter-attack—that's Fight. Or they'll shut down and shut up—that's Flight.

I have witnessed both of these natural reactions in both Paddy and myself during arguments. It is useful to understand that our bodies were made to face great adversity and gifted with adrenaline that would increase our chances of survival if threatened. Those gifts don't work as well in the modern era, where verbally negotiating or working through emotional issues doesn't pose the same threat as facing wild animals that want to eat us. But our bodies do not know the difference.

When we start to get worked up just a tiny bit, most of the blood rushes from our brains to our bodies preparing us for the Fight or the Flight. This is exactly opposite of what we need in those situations, and that's why the repeat-back strategy is go great. It slows us down and makes us focus on what our partner is actually saying. You cannot listen and also create a strategy to demolish your opponent, nor can you shut down. The repeat-back creates space for you to better understand one another.

Finally, **never withhold your attention.** And remember, there are negative consequences of withholding your attention from you partner—and they're worse than a shitty vacation. If you don't listen attentively to your partner, you risk him feeling insignificant and ignored. And that goes for anyone else in your life too! Attentive listening is a life skill. WORK at becoming a good listener, and it will pay off—*especially if you and your partner are opposites!*

Get on the Same Page

Now, let's talk about one area where it can be especially difficult to be opposite from your partner: the big decisions that drive your life. When dealing with something that is going to impact your lives every day, like how you manage your money, it's not enough to say, "You do you, and I'll do me." You've both got to work toward getting on the same page in a functional way—by which I mean that neither you nor your partner has to change *per se*; you just have to find a solution in the middle that you can both adhere to so you can get stuff done.

Let's use money as an example since that can be a huge point of contention for couples. [10]

If you are anything like Paddy and me, the way you view and handle money is different—maybe even opposite. How can the two of you get on the same page financially?

First, you've got to get on the same page at a very high level. Start with your values. What are your top values? How do those values translate to your top goals? Then, how do your values and goals translate to your finances and financial goals? There is a worksheet called The Financial Same Page at the end of the book that can help you work through these questions. It's all trickle-down economics from there (ha ha).

When Paddy and I were first married, our top values were each other and raising our children. These values

---

10   Olivia Mellan dives deeper into the statistics of finances and couples. She would say even if you happened to couple up with someone who shared the same viewpoints on money—with the same financial profile, it's likely one of you will adapt in order to maintain the relationship. (Take the quiz at https://www.moneyharmony.com/moneyharmony-quiz, and it will give you information about your "money personality" and information about her books, all of which are great resources if you are struggling in this area)

translated to goals of having a home to live in with plenty of food on our table and clothes on our backs. It meant spending quality time together. We wanted our children to have good educations all the way through high school, and we wanted to be able to pay for their college should they decide they wanted to go. We also wanted to retire, preferably early if possible. Financially it meant we both needed to work to pay for our home, food, clothes, and a few dates a month, plus have enough to start saving for college for the kids and retirement. Boom! Here was the shared foundation for our financial life.

By creating our shared vision for the life we wanted to have together, we created the "same page" from which we could craft our mutual approach to money. Our budget centered on (and stemmed from) our values and goals. From there, we could build out individualized approaches that would make it easier for both of us to adhere to the plan. We factored in some "free" money for each of us. We agreed to a one-time spending limit. If one of us wants to purchase something over a certain dollar amount, we both need to sign off on the expense.

It is a good idea to sit down on a regular basis (annually works for us) and realign to ensure you're living according to your agreed values. I don't remember having any high-level, value- and goal-based discussions about our finances in the years before our break-up. We bickered over how we were spending money, but it wasn't as urgent as the conversations we had when we didn't actually have any money. Had we maintained the discipline to continue those discussions, they could have led us to talk through our priorities (which we agreed were our children and each other). Maybe we could have made adjustments before reaching our breaking point?

It is also a good idea to go through your budget and track how you are doing. Are you following the budget and staying within the guidelines you created? It is good to do this at least monthly (weekly is ideal) and make adjustments as necessary. And when it comes to big financial decisions—large purchases, accumulating debt, or selling assets—you need to find the same page. Agree to stay in the conversation until you can come to a creative and mutually agreeable solution. And, yeah, it may be that it takes multiple weeks or months before you come to an agreement, but just keep talking until you get there. KEEP UP THE ENDEAVOR! It is a healthy and necessary part of your marriage and the longer you do it, the easier it will be. (Really.)

HE SAID: THE IRRELEVANCE OF THE MINUTIA

So many times in our conversations we can fall off of the same page by arguing over the minutia of how we got there. Sam and I have spent ten minutes arguing over which wrong turn made us late. It's an unnecessary argument. It doesn't matter. We are at the destination.

There is no page to get on other than what to do next.

The same thing goes for when Sam and I are already on the same page, but we disagree as to how we got there. For example, we sometimes disagree on how to do something. "I usually do it this way," Sam will say. "Yes that is fine," I might respond, "but I am more comfortable doing it this way and here is why." The same page was that we both wanted the project done. It is done. Yet here we are arguing about the differences within our specific techniques. "Keep your eyes on the prize" is something Sam likes to say, and I think it's a good rule of thumb here. Do not get sucked into the differences of the details. Most of the time they do not matter.

But how do we know who is right?

This is a huge pitfall in most relationships. For some reason, we all seem to have an inherent desire to be right. For some, it is so important that you ignore that you were on the same page and continue the disagreement just because you didn't hear the words "you were right." Disagreements are fine; we will all have them. But you have to defuse them before they turn into harsh words. If that happens, then you have a whole other can of worms to deal with. We'll discuss that can of worms in depth in a later chapter (When Shit Goes Down).

So here you are, in a fight. But why? Was it just because you needed to be right? What if you were wrong but still got everything you wanted, would that be okay? That is what recognizing the same page is all about. If you have to say you were wrong to stay on the same page with your partner, who cares? Do it. Say this with me, "Okay, okay, you are right, I must have misunderstood." That wasn't so hard, was it? And look, here we are, on the same page!

Recognize your goal: getting on the same page as your partner. Then ignore how you got there, do not get sucked into the minutia of the surrounding details and do not worry about who was right. That is the best way to stay on the same page.

CHAPTER 6

STOP, DROP, AND ROLL

You probably recall the three most basic rules of fire safety. They've been drilled into most of since we were kids and are easily summed up in a catchy phrase: Stop, Drop, and Roll.

When you are on fire: You need to STOP! The instinct is to run, but this only feeds the flames with much-needed oxygen. Then you need to DROP: literally, drop to the ground. Then you ROLL on the ground to extinguish the flames. If you didn't learn this in school or elsewhere, you're welcome. Now you know what to do should you ever catch on fire.

Obviously, we don't catch on fire as a result of being in a relationship, but we do have traumas that will burn us up physically and/or emotionally, completely change our worlds and the way we live in them. We're talking about trauma, tragedy, injury, sickness and death. We're also talking about other issues like depression and discontent.

How you handle turmoil that erupts in your life or the life of your partner can either make or break your relationship. If you live long enough, you can guarantee you will have to deal with major emotional issues as friends and family members pass, as we all must. You will be faced with your own injuries and illness as well as those of your partner. If you don't weather these storms gracefully, you can count on more storms and more difficult times to come. However, get this right, and the bond between you will be as strong as any love bond that exists. It will be a giant leap on your way to Pragma and Agape love.

SHE SAID: WHEN THE SKY IS FALLING...

It was our daughter's birthday and we were out on our boat in a lake in the mountains, wake boarding, surfing, water skiing, and just hanging out with close friends and family. It was a perfect day. Blue skies, sunshine, great company. Then my parents called. I ignored the call the first time thinking it likely had something to do with the dinner plans we had the next night, but after the third call, I answered. It was my mother. She was crying.

"Daddy is dead!"

"What?" I asked her not really wanting her to repeat what she just said but also not sure I heard her correctly.

"Daddy is dead!"

My dad had died suddenly that afternoon watching television on the couch while my mom was out running errands. I was devastated. My dad was not only my dad but had become one of my best friends over the past few years. We started a few businesses and took up motorcycle riding together. In fact, we had just returned from a motorcycle trip to Nevada only three days before.

Paddy scooped me up in his arms when I collapsed. He then carried me for weeks. He took care of everything while I grieved and managed all of those things needing attention when someone close to you passes. He gave me anything I needed from him—not just the logistics of ensuring our kids were cared for and keeping our household running, but also all those things I needed from him to help me get through the tragedy. One minute I needed him to hold me, and the next minute I needed space and time to process. He never judged or criticized. I always felt loved. I am eternally grateful, and his unwavering compassion created a bond and a trust that was reminiscent of Storgē love and the embodiment of Agape love. Paddy literally did everything.

This was what we call *Stop, Drop, and Roll*. And the story of losing my dad is both an extreme and a clear example of it in action.

When you realize your partner is distraught, struggling, crying, upset, or things are not okay, your job is to STOP whatever you are doing, DROP everything, and ROLL with them to help to put out the fire.

When talking about death or loss, "Rolling" means to ease the suffering or soothe your partner's distress as best you can. So in my example, Paddy first physically held me while I was on the phone with my mother and while

I cried uncontrollably for many minutes after that. I'm not sure he even knew what was wrong at that point; he just knew something was upsetting me terribly.

However, Rolling is rarely as simple as dealing with the immediate emotions. There are almost always other steps that need to be taken to cope with distressing situations. Sometimes it will be as simple as a conversation where you engage in active listening with your partner. Other times it will be much more involved, with multiple ongoing conversations, emotional outbursts, and sometimes it may even require life changes.

Tragedy always leaves us changed, and that goes for our close relationships as well. It seems these events or traumas can either tear people apart or pull people together. However, there are a few things that will help you to survive these lows when you are the helping partner.

Eliminate judgment and criticism. When your partner is struggling, judging them for it, deciding if it is right or wrong, good or bad, or whether they should or should not be struggling is a complete waste of time. It doesn't matter. What does matter is that they are hurting, and you love them and want to help them any way you can. If you feel yourself getting annoyed or edgy, ask yourself if you are judging or being critical. If your answer is yes, take a moment to identify the judgment or criticism and let it go. If you can master it, this technique will create more space for love and acceptance in both yourself and your partner.

Don't be afraid to ask your partner what they need. It's great when you can anticipate their needs, but often our instincts are more aligned with what *we* need or want. I recently heard a story of a husband who came to the funeral of one of his wife's close relatives and left to play golf immediately after it ended. She was deeply hurt, but he had no idea he'd done anything wrong—he had gone to the funeral, after all. That's why it's important to ask. Sometimes your partner won't know, and if that's the case, don't be afraid just to try some stuff. Sometimes, especially during times of tragedy, just being physically present can go a long way.

Don't take it personally if your partner is not as appreciative as you hoped (or at all). Often we are not at our best during difficult times. Emotions are on the surface and raw, we may be experiencing more pain than we ever thought we could endure, and it's possible our patience and gratitude aren't where we want them to be. If your partner snaps at you, know it has nothing to do with you and don't let it get you down. As Paddy would say, "Don't own it!"

Listen, listen, listen. And then listen some more. There's a good chance your partner will just want you listen, and talking through the issue may reduce or relieve some of his or her pain. Honestly, have you ever come out of a conversation thinking, "JEEZ, that guy listens too much"? Um, nope. I've never heard that. Ever. Everyone loves a good listener.

If your partner asks for your help or tells you what they need, make every effort to do those things. There are many people who say asking for help is the most difficult thing to do in a relationship, so when your partner asks for help, realize it may not be easy for them. Don't take it lightly. And how great is it not to have to guess! Take advantage of the advantage.

Don't give up! Don't go passive and stop trying if and when it seems like nothing is helping. Your partner needs you to keep trying!

On the flip side, there are also things you need to know as the partner receiving help:

Let your partner help you. I know a couple who went through a situation similar to Paddy's and mine. Her father died, and she was also devastated. Her husband loves her very much and tried his very best to help her. To hear her tell it, he did everything right—but she couldn't accept his help. She virtually shut him out, and it nearly cost them their marriage. If you find yourself refusing help, support, or love from your partner, STOP doing that! There are few things more hurtful than not allowing your partner to help you. Know that you might be hurting them when you refuse their help.

Don't be afraid to ask for help or tell them what you need. Paddy often touches me—not just when I'm struggling, but all the time—and he steps it up a notch when he is worried about me or trying to comfort me. I've learned this is his way of helping, and I try to be as gracious as I can. Then there are times when I really don't want anyone to touch me, when what I need is to be left completely alone. And I can kindly say to Paddy, "Baby, I love you, and I love your touch and your company, but I think what I need right now is just to be by myself." Because Paddy doesn't "own it," he takes the input gracefully and gives me the alone time I need.

Sometimes the struggles aren't tragedy; sometimes it is a longer-term dissatisfaction, minor distress, or mere annoyance. The good news is these strategies work anytime you need help or need to give help.

HE SAID: LEAN ON ME

I was having a conversation with my buddy Pat about his marriage. He and his wife Kim have been married more than twenty years and, according to Pat, have never come close to calling it quits. They chalked it up to one reason: If Kim ever became frustrated or unhappy with their relationship, Pat would stop and prioritize her frustration and unhappiness until she felt better about their situation. It didn't matter how busy or preoccupied he might've been, if his wife was unhappy, it was a Stop, Drop, and Roll situation. Pat recognized that Kim and his family was his *Why,* his meaning of life, and if that was broken it needed to be fixed ASAP. Everything else would wait. "What's the point of everything else if your wife and kids are unhappy?" he asked me.

I couldn't have said it better myself.

The truth is that Stop, Drop, and Roll is not quite so easy as Pat makes it sound. It's complicated and requires understanding, patience and well-timed empathy.

Most men have a deep-seated need to fix broken things. Especially those who are self-made or leaders. We are natural-born problem solvers. We don't like it when stuff is broken, incompatible, or out of whack, so we try to fix it. (Many women right now might be wondering, "If this is true, then why is the garage door still broken after three years of limited function?" Well just because we like to fix things doesn't mean we are all handymen.) The things we like to fix usually have to do with people. That's why our teams are usually so strong.

Speaking for myself, I know that when Sam or the kids have problems I tend to immediately swoop in and try to FIX the problem for good. However, that is not what is always needed. Often the need is that of a more empathetic and listening nature and can't be fixed overnight. Some things may take months.

The second time Stop, Drop, and Roll popped up this year, was a completely different scenario. It was a situation where this strategy was critical, but the person I was talking to had no idea.

My good friend Ernest, who has had a couple of failed marriages, was imparting wisdom to a younger mutual friend Ryan, who had just gotten engaged. At the time I thought this hugely hypocritical. Without hearing his message, I made an immediate negative judgment.

That error on my part can be discussed in another book, called *I Was Wrong. AGAIN!* Fortunately for me, I later had a discussion with Ryan and he told me what Ernest had related.

Ernest, he said, told him that his most recent wife was everything he wanted and that the relationship was awesome. He said that she adored him and that he got "charged" by that adoration. He was hugely grateful, usually reciprocated and they were very happy. Then one day her thirteen-year-old dog died. (She had the dog well before Ernest had come along and since she had no kids of her own, the dog was "her baby.") She went into a depression and shut down.

When that happened the adoration stopped, Ernest was no longer the center of her universe. She was not filling up his tank and giving him the "charge" he had come to expect from her. So he immediately went into "fix it" mode. He applied empathy for a short while but then became impatient with her depression: "It was just a dog." "You need to snap out of it." "I am a person who is right here and needs you." He was no longer getting that "charge" from her, and now he was hurting.

Technically this story is a two-part lesson, as this is a classic case of relying on someone else to give you fulfillment instead of yourself. You have to love yourself first, as you well know by now.

In the end, they were not able to make it work. According to Ernest, she changed and was no longer the person he married. Several years later he realized the

HUGE mistake he had made. He had used her adoration to validate himself (fill his tank). When it stopped, he became restless and grouchy and could not see how badly she needed him. He couldn't set it all aside and be there for her for a while. He had let her down when she needed him most. It was a powerful lesson in Stop, Drop, and Roll that he had learned years too late.

A Note on Grief

For most of you, like me, your partner is a very large part of your *Why*.

Recognizing this we must also remember that we need to always be there for them and never give the perception that we are not. Sometimes being there means that we have to let grief run its course and do anything we can just to help them feel loved and supported. We may need to put other things on hold while we are focusing on being there. We need to be there, knowing we may not be able to "fix" it. We need to be there, knowing that it will take time—possibly more time than we think. We still need just to be there. Completely.

To sum it all up, to me, Stop, Drop, and Roll means two things:

1. If something is broken, you stop everything and fix it.
2. If a person is broken (e.g. grief), you stop everything and *don't* try to fix it. Just be there.

Simple, right?

CHAPTER 7

BE YOUR PARTNER'S BIGGEST FAN

Have you ever met a couple and immediately felt envious of their relationship? As awesome as we are together, we have friends with a seriously enviable marriage. Their names are Bob and Usha. They have been married for almost thirty years, but they are so sweet and tender to one another you'd think they were still in the honeymoon phase. Whenever we're around them, we always reflect on how they take such good care of one another. They communicate with such grace and patience; they frequently ask each other if they are okay or whether they need anything from one another. They are often holding hands or snuggling.

They also seem to be each other's biggest fans. They laugh the loudest at each other's jokes, they compliment each other, and they point out the strengths of their partner to others. It never comes off as bragging as these are two of the most authentic, giving, spiritual people you'll ever meet, it just comes off that they think the world of each other. You also get an overwhelming feeling of how grateful they are to have each other.

That, in a nutshell, is what it means to be your partner's biggest fan.

SHE SAID: BE YOUR PARTNER'S LOUDEST CHEERLEADER

This is something I strive to be for Paddy. I endeavor to be his biggest fan, and I think it makes me a better wife because I'm always looking for the good stuff he does to compliment and share with others. I want to lift him up and it must be working because recently Paddy's cousin Dan said, "Sam, you talk about Pat like he's the smartest guy in every room, and you go further than that. You do more than compliment him; you fiercely advocate for him if you feel he is being slighted or treated unfairly." He went on to say we also compliment one another's ideas, even if we don't agree with them.

I say toot your partner's horn! Toot it loudly and proudly! Don't miss out on an opportunity to tell people how awesome they are because it will make you feel good and it will make them feel good.

HE SAID: I LIKE IT WHEN SHE TOOTS MY HORN. HEH, HEH...

SHE SAID: CAREFUL WITH TEASING AND NEVER TALK SHIT

Some couples, us included, tease each other. There is nothing wrong with teasing, as I would consider this to be part of Ludus love. It can be cute and endearing as long as it's described in a light of amusement and admiration. I think the things we love and miss about someone often are not their blaring strengths but idiosyncrasies and habits that make them uniquely themselves.

But there are times when teasing isn't a good strategy—and that is a delicate tightrope to walk. If you decide to tease your partner, watch their face. Are they smiling? No smile, no more teasing. And frankly, I think the same rule should apply even if your partner isn't in the room. Before you make a comment about your partner to someone else, consider: "Would this make my spouse stop smiling if they heard it?" If your answer is yes, you probably shouldn't say it.

I recently met the new wife of a friend of mine. As we were chatting—just the two of us—I asked her if she had ever met my husband, Paddy. She said she didn't think so and I said, "I can't wait until you meet him! He's fun!"

Her response took me a little by surprise: "I'm so glad you said that! I have so many friends and know so many women who have nothing nice to say about their husbands. I don't get it! I mean, you married the man, don't you have anything nice to say?" The more I thought about it later, the sadder her comment made me feel.

When I was a teenager, I read an article in a fashion magazine that said the fastest and easiest way to make friends is to find something in common, and a good place to start is by complaining about something. The advice stuck with me because it was one hundred percent right. Unfortunately, talking shit actually does work as a strategy to kindle kinship. However, it also demonstrates and then continues to encourage negativity. I don't know about you, but I don't need any more negativity in my life—and don't want it in my marriage—so I don't use that strategy to make friends.

AND, I think this strategy sucks even more if you are talking shit about your partner to gain closeness with a friend. Don't get me wrong, I've talked plenty of shit, and I've talked plenty of shit about Paddy—especially when we were on the brink of divorce—but you'll be hard pressed to hear me talk shit about anyone anymore. It is bad form on so many levels.

For one thing, talking shit severely erodes trust! Don't be fooled by thinking it just erodes trust with your partner only if you get caught or what you said gets back to them. Even if the person you are talking to doesn't consciously think or say this, deep down there is a part of them that is wondering what you might say about them when you are not in their company. This is

ESPECIALLY true if you are talking trash about your partner! Think about it. If this is the person you've committed your life to, the person you are supposed to love and trust the very most in the entire world, and they are also supposed to love and trust you the very most in the entire world, what kind of a chance does anyone else in your world have?

Don't ever talk poorly about your partner to anyone else. If you need advice, you can speak in confidence with a close friend but stick to the facts. If you stray from the facts the advice won't be any good anyhow.

If you won't be your partner's biggest fan, who will? You should be their biggest fan—and the way you do that is you continually focus on all the good stuff. His fabulous smile, her amazing sense of humor, his dedication to his family, her consideration of people's feelings. Forget about the flaws—we all have them—and since what you focus on gets bigger, do you want more flaws or more good stuff?

An amazing magical thing happens when you and your partner are each other's biggest fans. You start to relax into is this very comfortable feeling knowing your partner has your back. Wondering if anyone will ever really love you never crosses your mind again. You become more comfortable in your own skin knowing the person who knows you the very best, loves you the very most!

HE SAID: MY *WHY* DEFINED AND EXPLAINED

We have mentioned the term your *Why* before and will likely refer to it again. For me, it is not as complicated to define as it is to explain, but I'm going to give it a shot in this chapter. By definition, my *Why* are Sam and the kids. It is my mom and my dad, my close friends and those I care most about. These are my loved ones. They are my reasons why I do what I do. They are my biggest fans and I am theirs.

Now that I've defined, let me try to explain:

Sam is a songwriter and has been since before we met. She writes the most amazing songs that pull at your heartstrings and bring tears to your eyes. At our wedding, she surprised me by playing a song she wrote in place of her vows. It made me cry in front of my whole family, which is a testament to how important she is to me. I fancied myself a big strong man who was not easily rattled, but I had no problem showing her how incredible that song made me feel. I had appreciated her talent before, but there was no question after that moment I was going to be her biggest fan.

As fans, we all take some credit for the success of the ones we root for. We wear their jerseys, we put bumper stickers on our cars, we go to the concerts, and we buy the products. We are quick to remind people that we did not come from the bandwagon, that we have been there since the beginning. It is almost inherent that we want to brag about those things. They mean so much to us and we want other people to know that we are fans and that our support played a part in their success. At least that's what happens with me; I gush when I am proud.

While Sam's songwriting is awesome, there is so much more light that she brings to the world. If she never wrote or performed another song, I would still be right there standing in front of the metaphorical stage, staring up at her in speechless awe. She is giving, confident, introspective, and genuinely caring and all loving. I strive to one day be all that she has become.I will always be her biggest fan. You may be gagging right now after all of that, but it is how I feel. I am so proud that I get to play a part in her life. See? Gushing.

We have had twenty-one years to get to where we are, but I can't say I was always Sam's biggest fan. I am certain that during our year apart I was the guy hauling a bag of rotten tomatoes to her concert. Ready to lob a volley of heckles and boos mixed with airborne nightshades at her. I had forgotten who she was and most importantly who I was. As our partner's biggest fan, we need always to remember who they are and who we are. But it does take some time. We have to learn to accept the losses as much as the wins, maybe more so, because that is when they need us most. It is when you endear yourself as a true fan. It doesn't happen overnight; it grows with your love. To be the biggest fan you have to become and remain truly devoted.

Our spouses, partners, and families are the ones who will always be there for us, and we need to be there for them the best way we can. I want to make them proud of me. I want to set a good example for them. I want them to pay it forward by carrying those same virtues within themselves. I want to arm them with everything they need to succeed any way they desire.

While it can be an incredible validation when those we root for achieve success, it should not be what we use to validate our loved ones. Often there is no measurable achievement, and there will be times when those we root for take some steps backward. Being a true fan—the biggest fan—is about complete support of and faith in those loved ones. Win or lose we need to be by their side supporting them any way we can. It is about love. This love does not fall into a defined love language, and while it is most described by Agape love, it is only unconditional until it is not. It is a love that must come with the territory of having relationships.

My *Why*, in essence, is to be the biggest fan. I am proud of those I love, and I want them to be proud of me. Almost everything I do, including the things that are for me, is aimed at growing and enhancing that love.

CHAPTER 8

BEFORE SHIT GOES DOWN— DEFUSE THE SITUATION

Some fights are attempts to get on the same page about decisions, and others are about getting on the same page when you don't need to be on the same page. Many fights, deep down, are disagreements about fulfilling each other's needs. Sometimes just recognizing which scenario a discussion falls into can begin to defuse a situation.

It goes without saying that the best way to fight is to avoid fighting altogether. If categorizing the type of discussion doesn't defuse it, this chapter includes some other tactics we use to avoid fights.

SHE SAID: YOU HAVE THE POWER

You love your partner and every communication with him or her is an opportunity to express love.

When I first heard this idea, I thought it was total woo-woo bullshit—completely unrealistic. What if Paddy isn't expressing love to me? What if he is doing and saying hurtful, insensitive things? Isn't it my right (maybe even my obligation) to say and do hurtful things back, so he knows how bad it feels? The Bible says an eye for an eye.

There is something funny about "hurtful, insensitive things" ... the first of which is that we all perceive "hurtful" and "insensitive" differently. It's a very subjective thing. The things I feel are hurtful may not rattle you at all and vice versa. And since this is so very subjective, often a person's intention is misunderstood. Sometimes people say and do things without any intention of harm. If you knew the intention was not to be hurtful or cause you harm, would that affect how you felt about it?

As the receiver of messages (verbal and nonverbal) you perceive to be hurtful, you should consider that you may be misconstruing the intention and give the deliverer of the message the benefit of the doubt. Tell yourself you are not under attack because even if you are, your best reaction is the same.

Here is the thing: If you believe someone intends to hurt you, you will likely have a very negative feeling about it, and you will also likely have a very negative reaction. However, neither of these things will help you or the messenger or your relationship. A negative reaction now also pulls the messenger down, and now you both feel like shit.

The thing here is, you may not always get to decide how you feel about something because often emotions well up quickly before we even really know what is happening. (Although I will tell you the more you practice thinking "I am not under attack" and giving people the benefit of the doubt, your feelings will also start to change. It takes some time but it rewires your brain, and soon you won't even have those negative feelings because you no longer feel attacked. Even if you are being attacked—because as you'll learn, it's completely irrelevant.)

You ALWAYS get to DECIDE how you will react to anything and everything in your life.

Think about that. YOU ultimately are all powerful. You have the power to create a downward spiral of crappy annoyance, anger, hurt, and sadness in yourself and others by the way you choose to REACT or you can create a non-issue or even a positive experience for you both.

Paddy and I used to have some pretty raunchy fights, and it was partly due to my anger management issues. (Okay, fine, it was *mostly* due to my anger management issues.) I used to think that having temper tantrums was an entirely effective method of communication. I blame my grandfather who had a bad temper and whose last name was Temple, and thus my anger outbursts were aptly called the "Temple Tantrum" in our household. I'm embarrassed that it took me so long to figure out that what I was doing wasn't healthy for my family or myself.

My outbursts and the subsequent reactions were bad— we're talking screaming, slamming of doors, slamming of drawers, sleeping on the couch, airing out our shit in front of friends, and more. Paddy and I had so many disagreements—because we are opposites—and had no idea how to work through them. And it was usually me on the offensive launching attacks. He'd spent too much money; he wasn't spending enough time with me; he wasn't spending enough time with the kids; he didn't take out the garbage. I was extremely critical of him, just as I was of myself.

Early in our marriage, Paddy would vehemently defend himself, either through denial or by telling me it just wasn't important. There was also the tactic of launching his counterattack—usually founded on how I was yelling at him and the number of "fucks" I had said in the past thirty seconds.

As we've gotten older, he sometimes uses humor to defuse my anger. I remember screaming on and on and looking over at Paddy, who had removed his shirt, pushed his belly out as far as he could and was rubbing it gently. He looked into my eyes sadly and said in all seriousness, "You're upsetting the baby." We both started laughing, and by the end of our giggle session, I couldn't even remember what we were talking about. This doesn't always work, I will warn you, and if I was really on the warpath or the topic was very sensitive, this would have backfired and I would have likely added to the "fuck you" count as I stormed out of the room.

And now? Well, I rarely get mad because I know what a waste of time and energy it is. That was all it took was for me to change my behavior completely. I realized it was ineffective, meaning there were better and more efficient ways of getting things done. Not only that but there were other ways I could handle it, and use the situation (and my reaction to it) to build and grow our love instead of ripping it down. Here are some tactics you can use:

Ignore bad behavior. This means exactly what it says. I used to say a lot of mean and awful things when I had my Temple Tantrums. I wanted Paddy to feel bad. When he would react, it would fuel the fire and, in my mind, justify saying more bad things. When he didn't respond and acted like I hadn't said a thing, it confused me, and I would pause. The pause was usually enough for me to self-reflect and realize what a bitch I was being.

Let it go. Sometimes Paddy doesn't say anything, and he chooses to let it go—and when I say let it go, I mean he never talks about it again. Sometimes I would go "silent," and it seemed like I was letting it go but really I was putting it into my bag of ammo—adding another data point to help launch my next offensive attack. But Paddy truly lets it go.

Apologize. Other times he apologizes if he sees I'm upset about something. Sometimes he apologizes for what he thinks might have upset me and sometimes he can't apologize for anything because he doesn't know what he did wrong. So he simply says, "I'm sorry. I seem to have said or done something to upset you." This is a heartfelt apology; he looks into my eyes, maybe even touches my shoulder or grabs my hand. Not the snarky "sorry" you throw out because you feel like you have to do it. You have to mean it for this to work.

Get Curious. Other times Paddy gets curious about why I might feel the way I do and asks thoughtful questions about what I'm feeling at the moment. These questions are motivated by caring and real curiosity. I had found myself pretending to be caring and curious when I was just asking questions to lead Paddy to say something so I could "win" an argument or show him how wrong he was for feeling the way he did. At times my questioning was both accusatory and manipulative, and that is *not* how you do it. The intention of your questions is to show you care, learn more about your partner, build trust, and make your relationship a safe place to talk about your innermost feelings. It's scary at first, but *that* is what makes a relationship last as long as life does.

State your case gently, without accusing your partner. In some cases, if I might be getting angry and Paddy's emotions are in jeopardy of escalating, he might say, "I'm feeling attacked." In earlier days when I knew I was actually attacking him, this statement might have launched a full defensive, and then we would need to jump down to the section about how to fight.

However, nowadays my intention is never to attack him. I know attacking him never brings the results I want. The results I want are for me to feel loved and supported, for him to feel loved and supported, and for us to have a deep, beautiful relationship. We both recognize our disagreements deep down are often really discussions about fulfilling each other's needs. So now when he says this to me, it leads to an immediate apology, saying I'm sorry because I did not intend for him to feel attacked. Then I try to find a better way to say what I need to say. Sometimes that happens right away, and other times it takes longer.

The other funny thing about "hurtful, insensitive things," particularly with our partners, is we believe they should *know* the things that hurt our feelings or make us angry. They should *know* when they are doing hurtful and insensitive things, right? But even after twenty years of marriage, I'm sometimes surprised by the things that make Paddy defensive, and I'm equally surprised by the things Paddy says and does that I take personally and allow to hurt my feelings.

Do not assume you know how your partner is feeling or that your partner knows how you are feeling—no matter how long you've been together. Instead of assuming, it is completely fair to ask your partner how he or she is feeling. Again, get curious instead. My tendency is still to judge if I am not intentional about the curiosity. Meaning, if I say something I think is funny to Paddy and he takes it very personally, I'll almost immediately judge him and say he is wrong for misunderstanding my intention. He should be giving me the benefit of the doubt, I'll think, and quit being so sensitive. But see, you can't, nor will you ever get to control what your partner does or how they react.

You can only control what YOU do, so quit judging everyone else for what they choose to do. Focus instead on YOUR part of what went down. Since you can only control yourself, focus on what you have said or done (or the way you said it or did it) and figure out what you could have done differently. There is power in this exercise, as you recognize that you don't need your partner to change their behavior; you can change yours and see what happens.

As an example, it used to be that when Paddy had something on his face, I would just wipe it off. For me, it was a way of showing love and nurturing—Storgē love, Act of Service, and Physical Touch—a trifecta! It was intimate too; because you would never do that to someone you didn't care about deeply. But sometimes, even if we were alone, Paddy would get upset about it. He'd seem hurt or angry which made zero sense to me. I was trying to help! So, despite his annoyance, I continued doing this for many years (and occasionally I still do it out of habit).

Then one day it hit me: why was I insisting on still doing it when I knew he didn't like it? It was in part was because I know he doesn't want to wander around with cheese in his beard, but it was as much because I felt like he was being stupid and I was being a loving wife. Nonetheless, I realized I don't want to do things that make Paddy feel bad, and so I changed my approach. Now I just tell him if he has cheese in his beard. It doesn't bother him and there is no skin off my back—I can kiss him or grab his hand or tickle his back, or myriad other things to show love and nurturing.

HE SAID: SOMETIMES IT'S JUST ANNOYING

I don't know why but it makes me feel I like a little kid who can't take care of himself, or a person so far gone they need someone to else take care of them. I know it is my choice to feel that way and a bigger person would choose to not act on that feeling. But sometimes shit is just annoying, and that is the way it is. So I prefer to be told that there is stuff on my face rather than be mothered. I guess Storgē love is something I am not always ready to receive.

HE SAID SOME MORE: DON'T OWN IT, OWN IT, BE OVER IT, AND PATIENCE

Tell me if this sounds familiar: Sam said, did, or didn't do something in a way I didn't like. I then either snapped back at her (Fight), which kicked off a new shit storm because I made her feel unsafe and attacked, or I became superbly annoyed and shut down or walked away (Flight). Flight, in my opinion, can be a worse option, with one exception: "putting yourself in timeout," as Sam calls it. Flight only works if you are taking some time to calm yourself down.

Unfortunately, however, flight for me used to look a lot more like this: "I can't believe she said that. Fuck her." I'd then walk away and immediately start telling myself stories about why the whole thing was Sam's fault. That kind of storytelling typically does little more than throw gas on the fire. And, unfortunately, it's usually false. So now I have taken something she did, or said, or didn't do and propelled it to an entirely different level, tossed gas on it and started an inferno.

Sam might just have had something in her eye and was not rolling her eyes at me. She might not have been thinking at all when she made that comment and likely has no idea why it pissed me off. And no matter how many times I forget, she still can't read minds.

It's the story I tell myself that actually causes the deeper hurt. That is what we need to eliminate. I call that, "Don't Own it!" which essentially means do not take any of it personally.

Don't Own It

I used to own Sam's shit for days. She would come home after a long trip and be tired. I was excited and happy to see her. When she didn't show the same excitement and instead snapped at me because she was tired, I would take it personally. Not only that, but I would also build out an epic story about it, with varying plots and twists and several possible surprise endings. Then I'd sulk off and be mad while Sam was left wondering what was up with me.

Days later, and after my pouting prompted her to keep asking what was wrong, I might tell her. Even if she acknowledged her bad behavior, Sam was usually completely blown away that I was still hanging on to it and would then get annoyed at me for being such a "baby." The whole process was massively unhealthy and usually based on something silly that I then compounded with fiction I had built in my head.

But that is what can happen when you "own someone else's shit."

I was talking with a friend a few days ago, and he expressed that he had been angry with his spouse about something "unnecessary" she said. She had asked him not be an ass when he came home because the house was in a rare state of peace with the kids. Her goal was to keep the peace and have a happy family. He took it as a personal attack. He became annoyed that she would think this about him. "That was the old me," he said. "She should recognize that I have not been that guy for several months."

Well, there are a few things wrong with that approach. The first being his negative ownership of what she said. He should have just said "No problem babe, see you soon," then hung up and taken a minute to calm down and recognize her intention to keep the peace and the family happy. Sure she could have delivered it much better, but we have to give each other a bit of room in this process. We will never be perfect, and we can't expect our spouse to be either.

Since he chose to get upset and demand an apology, this well-intentioned attempt at keeping the peace now turned into something different. He added a whole new chapter to the story by insisting that she recognize his efforts at improvement and not say something that acknowledged his older bad behavior. He took it personally. He owned it. Again, no one is perfect, so even though we may slip and get offended at something our partner says (I still do), the important thing is to recognize it quickly and get OVER it. Preferably before we get home and anyone else notices!

Okay, Now OWN IT!

You do not have control over someone else's bad behavior. Rather than stew about being treated poorly (your story), instead look inside and see what triggers led up to the actions or words that made you upset. Then think about how you may have contributed. Take any ownership you can and be the first to apologize, then MOVE ON. Even if you have a perceived minuscule role, OWN it. "I am sorry if I may have said something to upset you earlier. You seemed very angry at me." Ninety-five percent of the time your spouse will immediately own their bad behavior too: "I am sorry, too. It wasn't you; it must be..." The other five percent of the time, it just takes more time.

No Matter What, BE OVER IT

The theme of this chapter for me is: Own it when it's yours; don't own it when it's theirs. And at some point, in both cases, be OVER it.

When I do slip up and start feeling hurt or annoyed, I like to catch myself before or right after I open my mouth and say out loud, "Aaaaaaaannnd I'm over it!" Then smile. Sam will usually just laugh and won't even ask what it was about or push me on my comment. We both have learned that by owning bad behavior and then being OVER it, "IT" is now behind us.

Being over it takes some work. Especially if you are like me and used to owning stuff. The easiest way for me to be over it is to run whatever IT is through a simple test where I ask myself two questions.

1. What exactly am I upset about?

Just asking this question and answering it to yourself truthfully can most times defuse the situation and enable you to get over it. That is because what we choose to get upset about may be a reaction to something completely different or an overreaction due to stress. If that's the case, acknowledge it, be a bit embarrassed, and you are done. Over It.

Other times it can be as simple as recognizing, "I am choosing to feel attacked and have become defensive." The action then is to either decide to stop feeling and acting this way or communicate how you're feeling to your partner. If it is the latter, just talking about it honestly can often reduce the feelings enough that you can be over it.

If not, most times a favorable response from your partner will give you enough. If the response was not enough for you, then you are likely either still owning it, or have missed an opportunity to own it. Once you acknowledge that, you will once again be equipped to be over it. If not move on to question two.

2. Why am I still upset?

Repeat question one.

Is it really that easy? No, not always, but most times yes. "Most times" is where I am now. And the truth is, the difference between "always" and "most times" is minuscule compared to where you started. High Five!

This might be a good time to talk about patience.

We often give the people we work with or people outside of our marriage a wide berth when it comes to our patience. Yet the people we love the most, such as our partner, get a narrow margin in which to operate.

We come home from work, tired and expect the family to recognize exactly where we are. (After all they know you better than anyone and *should* know how you feel and *should* know what to say or not to say...) WRONG. Our families deserve as much or more of that same patience we give others. If we bring that home, it will make an immediate difference in how we interact with those we care about the most.

Last year, I visited my dear friends Tim and Karen. They have been married over twenty years and are real marriage warriors. But, they were in a vicious circle when I visited. Tim had little patience, and Karen had no patience for his impatience. This meant they were short with each other frequently and that their love was on a downward curve.

It was largely because Tim was not focusing on his *Why*. While I was confident that Karen would come around as soon as Tim started to remember and focus on that, she was giving back what she was getting for two reasons. First, she was annoyed at him for being short with her, and second (and more importantly), she knew why his fuse had been so short lately and was worried about him working too hard. That worry and recognition was also manifesting itself as anger. But no way did Tim see that at the time; I wouldn't either.

Tim is in charge of sales for a very successful company. He has to manage a sales and marketing force of all types of personalities, every day. That requires a lot of patience. When he comes home, it takes very little for him to become annoyed or lose patience with Karen. He is starting to recognize that but has not done anything to change it. Conversely, Karen is so used to getting little patience from him that she, in turn, gives him about the same or less. After more than two decades of marriage, this should not be. But it is also easy to do. We have all been there. The good news is it is just as easy to fix that vicious cycle as it is to fall into it.

It begins with patience.

First, we must agree that patience is a critical element to making a relationship work. We should also recognize that patience is precious in just about every other facet of life. When you catch yourself snapping at or being short with your partner, ask yourself what other things have been draining your energy and patience. Do those things deserve to take precedence over your partner in life?

That's when it's time to step back and analyze what is important to you. *What is it all really about? Is there an endgame?* Usually, the endgame is that we are doing it to provide for our family and set up some financial stability now and for the future. Right? Well, if your family is important enough to sacrifice for at work, then they should be every bit as important when you get home. I know you're tired and you probably just want to relax, but *don't get lazy* just because you crossed your patience threshold.

Your family deserves just as much effort (or more) as you apply at work or outside of the home. If you can take a raft of shit from a client, coworker or superior in stride, ride it out and come out of the situation on the high ground, then there is no reason you can't come home and do the same thing. You just need to set your intention before you walk through the door. The same way you do for the sales team or your friends.

Do what I do: Take a minute in the driveway. Remember your *Why*. Remember they deserve the best you can give MORE SO than anyone else. Then take a deep breath, walk through the door and give it to them.

Remember we are not perfect. You WILL forget this step and likely many other things we talk about in this book. I know I do, every day. But that doesn't mean we can't continually try and get better and better as we strive for mastery. Love your lovable self and try harder at every opportunity. Bring your A game as much as possible.

I have another trick I use to get back into my A game before I walk into the house. I talk to myself.

I will pause for a minute here to give you a chance to recover from having your mind blown.

Yeah, I know that trick is nothing special, but the conversation I have with myself is the key. It goes a bit like this: "Whoa, Big Fella, whatchya doing? This isn't part of who you are, right? You're the guy who recognizes what's most important to him and brings his A game home for his family. Now turn around so no one can see.

Deep breath, Aaaaaannnd exhale. Okay, now turn back around and begin again."

Boom! My A game is back!

The fact is your partner is your biggest fan. He or she is also your *Why*. You need always to remember this and never give them a reason to boo. Be the backbone of your family and lead by example with your A game. Be kind, be loving, be supportive, and most importantly, BE PATIENT.

CHAPTER 9

WHEN SHIT GOES DOWN—FIGHTING BETTER

Even if you use every tactic listed in the previous chapter, fights still happen from time to time. But that doesn't mean you can't weather the argument, end it quicker, and resolve the issues that caused it. Here is what we do and why.

SHE SAID—GET YOUR HEAD RIGHT BEFORE OPENING YOUR MOUTH AGAIN

Typically, if things erupt into an argument or a full-on fight, it means we've let things get out of control, our emotions are high, our defenses are up, and we're in it. These are the steps I take to get out of it so we can work things out.

Put yourself in timeout. When things get heated or even when someone just gets annoyed and it escalates a tiny bit, you physiologically turn into a monkey. Your body and mind turn to Fight or Flight mode, as an uncomfortable amount of adrenaline starts pumping through your veins and the blood rushes out of your head and into your muscles, readying your body to take a swing or run away. Your brain isn't functioning at the top of its game in this state.

Without a little redirection, you are likely going to escalate the situation further needlessly. Sometimes redirecting means physically leaving the situation, sometimes it is requesting a pause in the conversation if you're somewhere like an airplane or a car where you cannot exit, and sometimes as you become more skilled in some of these techniques, this is a deep breath and a moment. However, the timeout happens, just make sure you wait until you feel calmer.

Stay in timeout until you figure out where YOU can take responsibility. Take a time out until *you* can figure out what *you* did wrong to contribute to the argument. It takes two to tango, so they say, and there is *always* something you did or did not do that contributed to the escalation of the situation. If you haven't figured out what you did wrong or what you could have handled better, you haven't been thinking about it long enough.

Forgive yourself. Once you know what you can take responsibility for, forgive yourself immediately for your contribution to the argument. Forgiveness doesn't mean forget or repeat; it simply means love yourself enough to know, "I messed up. I'm human. I love myself and know I am deserving of forgiveness for my mistake." Don't beat yourself up about what you did. Apologize for your mistake and commit to working harder. To quote Jenai Lane, "We're going for correction, not perfection." A crazy thing happens when you forgive yourself: You create the space and softness necessary to forgive your partner.

Forgive your partner. This moment of forgiveness isn't anything you verbalize; it is something you choose to feel. It simply means you love your spouse enough to know, "You messed up. You're human. I love you and know you are deserving of forgiveness for your mistake."

Some of you may be thinking, "But what if my partner isn't sorry, doesn't admit to their contribution to the argument, and isn't even asking for forgiveness?" This may sound very strange to many of you, but you don't forgive them for them, you forgive them for *you*. Holding grudges is horrible for you. It's a gross buildup of negativity that holds attention, space, and energy that could all be better used to create the life of your dreams, express more love, and find more happiness. So let it go. Forgiveness (not only of yourself but of others too) is a critical aspect of self-love. It puts you into a more open and loving mindset to take you to the next step. (Sometimes this is easier said than done, so we devoted a chapter to how to get to forgiveness and gratitude!)

The apologies, the analysis, and the make-up. Because our lives are so busy, Paddy and I will often let a fight blow over, and we'll leave the "post-mortem" for a time when we can be alone, relaxed and when we're sure each of us is ready to talk about it (meaning we've moved through all of the steps previous). So sometimes, even though we haven't officially "made up," we carry on with our lives, working hard to express as much love as we normally do. If you have truly forgiven yourself and your spouse, the make-up step is something to bring closure and a brilliant way to bring your relationship closer. (It also typically comes with great sex!)

This step requires some finesse if it is going to be handled properly and deliver the outcome we want instead of starting another fight or escalating the previous fight. So there are a couple of things we need to know going into the apologies and the analysis stage. There is a fantastic book about communication in difficult situations called *Crucial Conversations*, which we've mentioned numerous times. If you haven't read this book yet, read it. It is written in the context of doing business, but it applies to any and all conversations—especially emotional ones. To paraphrase, a couple of the critical concepts in this book in my words: Keep your eyes on the prize, stick to the facts, and stay curious. Let's take a closer look at each concept.

Keep Your Eyes on the Prize

Keeping your eyes on the prize is the idea of going into a conversation knowing what you want to get out of it. ... And I don't mean the petty things, like getting your point across or "winning" the argument. I mean the BIG things: what you want out of the communication and, ultimately, out of the relationship. This is the PRIZE you should keep your eyes on.

For me in my relationship with Paddy, I want to be loved! I want to feel valued, appreciated, cherished ... and I want the same for Paddy. I want our relationship and our love to last as long as our lives. This is the BIG thing I want from my communications with Paddy. Turns out holding this thought and intention when I am interacting with Paddy makes all of those interactions much more likely to yield that result than when I don't focus on it.

To go back to the beginning of this section: You love your spouse, and every interaction is an opportunity to express love. If your communication isn't in some way an expression of love, find a way to make it one.

Before you go into the apology and analysis of a fight, you need to get your head in the right place and set your intention. Your intention should begin with wanting your partner to feel both safe and loved. Make sure you are feeling loving towards your partner before you begin the conversation. It's not always easy, especially after a fight, but there is an exercise that I find particularly helpful in getting those bad feelings out in a constructive way. (I find it especially helpful if I'm having trouble getting through to forgiving Paddy or myself.)

Write down all the negative thoughts you have about your partner and the situation and then burn it. DO NOT leave these things lying around. Shred them, flush them—I find burning them particularly freeing—or otherwise dispose of them so they can never be read by another living soul. This is an opportunity for you to get your shit OUT.

Then, I fill an entire page with all the things I love and appreciate about my husband. If you're not in a great place currently, go back to when you fell in love and list all of those things. After an entire page, you should have some warm fuzzies going for your partner that will help get you in the right frame of mind.

Your other intention should be to come to a resolution—even if that resolution is to agree to disagree. A resolution with your partner will allow you to move forward together, but hopefully, it will bring a deepening of the relationship, a greater understanding of one another, and a better appreciation of each other.

Facts Only

When fights escalate, the culprit often is our judgments, the stories we tell ourselves about why someone did or said something or our assessment of what kind of person they must be to have done it in the first place. Exaggerations and generalizations—saying things like "you always" or "you never"—tend to bear some blame too. If you state only the facts when you are speaking, it helps disarm the conversation. If you ignore your partner's judgments, exaggerations, and generalizations and bring it back to the facts, it also helps disarm the conversation. Try to stick to the facts only when you are speaking but also when you are listening.

I've often said things like, "You were a total asshole," while we were trying to analyze a fight. *So. Not. Helpful.* While I might argue otherwise at that moment, that kind of assessment is not a fact. It's a judgment, my opinion of Paddy's actions or attitudes. It's much more productive to say something like, "You said I embarrassed you and left the table suddenly. You never came back and I was stuck with all of those people asking me what happened and why you left." These are facts.

Telling your partner how you felt as a result of what had happened is another useful set of facts. So I might also say, "It left me feeling very confused and uncomfortable because I didn't know what I'd done to embarrass you. I still don't feel like I understand. I also felt hurt and angry that you left me there." These are statements of fact about how you felt. H*owever, when you state the facts about your feelings, be very mindful of how you word it.* If you say, "You made me feel..." now you are assigning your partner blame for your feelings as opposed to taking responsibility for them. Instead, start with "I was feeling," "I felt," or "I feel," to differentiate your truths from universal truths.

Curiosity Kills Cats but Saves Relationships

I've brought up curiosity multiple times already, but it's valuable in the aftermath of a fight because it helps you get out of your own head and allows room for new ideas, paradigm shifts, and discoveries—not only about your partner but also about yourself.

We're Not Perfect Either...

Recently Paddy and I got into a big fight. We hadn't fought in quite some time (like maybe more than a year?), but then we found ourselves in the middle of a pretty heated exchange about—wait for it—driving. And it lasted for more than an hour! I think once we'd cooled off we were both puzzled by why we'd fought so intensely about something so petty. That is until we started tallying up what was happening in our lives. We were both going through significant job changes, our children had recently left the nest, we had moved twice the year before but weren't totally happy with our new place and were considering moving again. Our stress levels were extremely high with so many changes in recent months.

Sometimes you have to take the pulse of your lives. Take a little inventory of your respective stress levels. Are you in the middle of a job change? Are you moving? Has anything traumatic happened to you or your family?

We started calling this stress phenomenon, which had contributed to more than one argument, the "boiling point." During less stressful times our boiling point is higher, meaning we don't boil over until the temperature is very high. During more stressful times, it takes much less. And it's during these times that we need to be more gentle and loving to our partners and ourselves.

I learned how much my nitpicking of his driving really affected him (after twenty years) and he learned I really could shut my mouth in the car. Well, mostly. Correction, not perfection.

HE SAID: I AM AN EXCELLENT DRIVER

I have never been in an accident while driving the family. In fact, I have not ever been in an accident since we have been together. Sure I have backed into shit, but nothing that has ever yielded more than a scratch. You would think that would buy me a little credibility behind the wheel. But it doesn't.

I am not sure what it is about being behind the wheel of a moving vehicle that wipes away all of my fight defusing techniques, but I almost always get super defensive when Sam criticizes my driving. The argument she mentions above was exactly like that. We didn't resolve anything that night, but later by asking questions of both Sam and myself, we came to a resolution.

A question I had to ask myself was, "Why do I get so defensive?" My answer highlighted my perfect track record and lack of acknowledgment from Sam. So then

I asked her the question, "Why do you think you don't give me any credit for the thousands of trips I have completed safely?"

The answers are not as important as the realizations we both had. Mine was that I needed to stop getting so defensive. It has gotten me nowhere in twenty-one years and likely will never change. I try and thank her now when she criticizes my driving after I point out how stupid her suggestion was. Correction not perfection, right?

If You Booze, You Lose

If you are ever arguing after having some drinks, stop. It will likely never end well. Arguments can end well, as Sam explained, but when alcohol is involved, we are usually devoid of the ability to utilize all that we have learned. Alcohol twists reality in our minds and gives us a fictional view, while also imploring us to defend it passionately. But it is not true.

How many have had an ugly argument while buzzed on booze, then felt a bit embarrassed the next day when you realized how trivial it was? My hand is in the air right now. I can't even count the times this has happened to us. Fortunately, we have put most of it behind us, but I can say that drinking was usually a factor when we fought more regularly.

When you drink, your filter dissipates, and you start saying what you are thinking. Some of it may be honesty, but a significant part of it is tainted by misperception and the stories we have told ourselves, then amplified by alcohol. And when we go after someone else with a half-truth or fiction based on a misperception, they will go straight to defense mode and then counter attack with their own tales (especially if they're buzzed too).

It may be easier to say than do, but when alcohol is involved, you must agree to table the topic to a time when you are both more clearheaded. If your partner refuses to do that, remove yourself from the argument however you can. You can't win; no one can.

Is The Argument about Winning? And Other Questions to Ask Yourself

When I realize I have let things escalate to an argument, I usually start thinking about how I can get the hell out of it. I do this by asking myself a few questions. Then by asking Sam questions. The first question is: ***Is this about being right?*** Often it is and being right is about winning, so we stand our ground. But when you insist you are right, the other person gets defensive because you are effectively saying they are wrong.

On to the next question: ***Does it matter at all?*** Sometimes it is just stupid, and my answer is that I don't really care one way or the other. So in this instance, even if I think I was right, I'll bow out. "You know what, babe? I am sorry. It really doesn't matter enough to me to argue about it." Then, either concede the argument and let them "win," or ask them: ***What is it you want to achieve from this?*** Then give them that.

If it does matter to you and you are still in the argument, this then begs the question: Are we arguing about facts, or is my point of view based on opinion? You can get out of an argument by focusing on what is factual and then proposing a solution. If Sam and I are arguing over facts, one of us will usually suggest a bet to settle the disagreement. We have a standing bet that involves a back rub or a blowjob. "Fine, the usual?" "Deal!" This is when it's my favorite time to be right.

If the argument is based on opinion, know that you're unlikely to change your partner's mind right there and then. Usually, emotions are too high, and you're not talking about the same set of facts anyway—you're talking about your stories. If it is your opinion you are defending, acknowledge that either party could be right based on their view, and express a desire to avoid further confrontation on the topic. This creates a safe exit for both sides.

Other questions I ask myself go back to Don't own it, Own it, from the last chapter. *Am I owning something Sam said past its expiration date?* Many times arguments get escalated by something someone says that ignites more defensiveness. By being vulnerable and explaining what was said and how you feel, you can help wind down the argument. Sam will often say, "I did not intend to make you feel that way." At that point, I need to move on and no longer let what she said continue to influence the conversation. If I continue to own it, we will continue to argue.

I also ask myself the question: ***Is it possible I can take responsibility for something that has upset her?*** You are correct; I am talking about Own It. If I can take a deep breath, accept some responsibility, and then apologize for it, most arguments dissolve right there. ***Don't Own It*** and ***Own It*** are not only great tools to discourage an argument, but they are also helpful for getting out of an argument.

Lastly, try humor. Ludus is huge for me in avoiding confrontation. If I can recognize we are acting stupid and then divert the whole thing with some form of playfulness or random humor, we both win. Most of the time when I do that we both instantly recognize that we were being dumb and laugh about it instead. This is my second favorite outcome to ending an argument.

CHAPTER 10

THE GREEN-EYED MONSTER

Jealousy is, stated simply, insecurity. However, jealousy is a tough one for many people to work through. It seems to be deeply seated in our psyches, especially if we've experienced abandonment or betrayal. It also gets fed by our society as an unavoidable emotion that justifies atrocious acts. Even our justice system acknowledges fits of jealous rage—or "crimes of passion" which we now refer to as "temporary insanity"—as a justified defense for violent crimes including murder.[11]

We believe, as we've said a number of times in this book, that although you cannot control your emotions such as jealousy, you can control your actions.

Case in point: not everyone understands jealousy

---

11   This defense was first used by U.S. Congressman Daniel Sickles of New York in 1859 after he had killed his wife's lover, Philip Barton Key (http://www. murderbygaslight.com/2009/10/dan-sickless-temporary-insanity.html) which set a precedence for the "temporary insanity" pleas still used today.

because it just does not exist for some people. In our case, one of us knows jealousy all too well and has plenty of experience with it, and the other has very little understanding of it. We received some advice to eighty-six this chapter altogether because "it doesn't really belong with the rest of the book." Our guess is that person has not ever had to deal with that monster and likely never will. They fall into the camp that just doesn't get it.

The good news is we think we can shed some light on both sides of jealousy for you. Even if jealousy isn't something you experience much in your own life, you will at least understand it better so you can muster the necessary empathy that might help your partner. If you do know that monster and need a few tools to cage it away, hopefully, our advice will help.

HE SAID: CAGE THE BEAST; LOVE YOURSELF

I can speak to this topic from about fourteen years of living it. For me, it started with one bad experience. My quest for improvement would later teach me that the experience was a huge insecurity problem transferred to me by someone who also had massive insecurity issues. Of course, I had no clue then and was new enough to the game that I played right into it.

My first real relationship where the words "I love you"

got tossed around, did not take place till I was twenty-six. I know, I know, I was a late bloomer. I had lived with this girl for about four months when things started to feel wrong. There were clues and inconsistencies everywhere that she might not be telling me the truth about her other relationships. I prefer the truth, so when she was being inconsistent, I would call her on it. Then she'd accuse me of being an asshole or of being insecure.

She would have been right had not every single clue turned out in the end to be absolute fact. My gut told me early on that something was not right and that she was not being honest with me, but I hung on because I was steered into second-guessing that gut feeling. I stayed for almost a year. Not much time really, I agree. But when the time is spent planting deep seeds of jealousy and insecurity, it is plenty. I don't like blaming my bad behavior on others; it is MY behavior. I get that. I only bring up this relationship because I had never had an issue with jealousy that I know of before this happened.

The irony is that this girl used to get super jealous when it came to my female friends. I thought it was kind of cute at the time, but I now know that her jealousy came from knowing what she was doing with all of the guys she swore to me were "just friends." Anyway, that is where it all began, the backstory for my jealousy. That relationship left me bitter for years after our breakup. I had trust issues, (aka jealousy issues) which then impacted my relationship with Sam. She knew the backstory and for a while was empathetic. Sam even created a nickname for the old girlfriend that I won't repeat.

Fast-forward to my marriage with Sam. As you already know our marriage is a tale of two very different decades. In decade one I had trust and jealousy issues that helped erode our relationship as much as any other factor.

Sam, as you will read, has no concept of jealousy. She just does not understand it. While empathetic in the beginning, she was much less patient with my jealousy later on. Most relationships that have one jealous partner will go this way unless the beast is released. Releasing that green-eyed monster can be tough once you have experienced the pain of cheating (either emotionally or physically—there isn't much difference, as they are both usually tied to feelings for someone else and the lying that goes with them).

So the question is: How do I stop the monster and kill it forever?

My answer is that you may never kill it. Now, before you get pissed at me, hear me out! I say you might never kill it because the majority will not. I haven't. I have caged it though, and it is not getting out. I can still hear its cries from time to time. And now and then it might influence my thinking if I let it. I can feel its hand in my pocket fishing around for the keys to the lock... Whack! Get out of there!! And I'm back! So yes, those thoughts pop up from time to time and sometimes out loud. But I am quick to lock that thought away or say something like, "Oh shit that sounded insecure. Sorry, babe, ignore that."

Listen, bottom line, jealousy is insecurity. It is you telling yourself: I may not be good enough. It is you worrying that your partner might leave you for someone "better." Sometimes it is the fear of being alone and starting over. It means you need work on loving yourself.

The key for me to overcoming my jealousy was recognizing it is an insecurity that had a negative impact on my relationships. That was not who I wanted to be anymore. I wanted to be a person who has enough self-value/self-love that I don't worry about those things I have no control over. To know that no matter what someone else does or does not do, I will be good. For my relationship, it is not a question of trusting her or not trusting her. The choice you must make is to give one hundred percent trust. That is all you have control over.

To not trust someone is the end. You will never succeed in your relationship if you can't give it all of your trust. At some point, you must get there. The thoughts may rise up now and again, but you need to recognize them for what they are, give yourself love, and remind yourself of what you do have control over. Then do more of that.

No matter what happens. Jealousy is a beast that needs to be caged forever. Because even if the worst scenario happens and your significant other cheats and the relationship ends, you do not want to carry that baggage along with you into your next healthy relationship. It will serve nothing positive in that relationship, ever.

SHE SAID: MOSTLY I DON'T GET IT

I have to admit I don't really understand jealousy in the way it affects most people. Sure I'm jealous of things like Paddy's time. If I don't get my share of that, then I become resentful of whatever is dominating his time. But as far as the green-eyed monster of jealousy, I've never really had an issue with it.

Jealousy seems like such a waste of time and energy to me. I understand it is an emotion and you can't truly control your feelings as I've mentioned earlier, but you control can your actions. To me, jealousy is insecurity, and I find it annoying. I can tell you this in all clarity: Being jealous or showing your jealousy will never help your partner love you more and it cannot prevent them from cheating.

Using our experience as an example, after I started traveling, Paddy would ask me constantly if everything was okay, if there was anything I wanted to tell him, and if I was sure there wasn't anything going on I needed to tell him about. This was during the time I had many male friendships developing. I've always had male friends, so this was not unusual nor did I consider it to be threatening to our relationship.

I would tell him about my male friends and the friendships that were developing and the flirting that may have taken place, but it never seemed to appease him. He continued to ask those questions, focusing on what I might be doing wrong that was causing his discontent with our relationship as opposed to focusing on what he might be able to improve himself to get us back on track. (We were both guilty of that.)

I felt that, by continuing to ask me those questions, he was already accusing me of cheating. After months of feeling accused, I started to think, "Well, if he thinks I'm guilty of cheating anyhow, I might as well cheat because I'm already being punished for the crime."

If Paddy had not been so jealous and accusatory would I have had those emotional affairs? I don't know. I might still have had them. However, what I can tell you is that Paddy's jealousy was a wedge between us that made it difficult to navigate everything else. No matter how much I would tell him I loved him and nothing was going on, his jealous green-eyed monster wouldn't let him believe me.

If you're like me and jealousy isn't something you experience or understand all that much, focus on making yourself the very best partner you can be. Make the healthy parts of your relationship so strong that any weaknesses such as jealousy don't matter. Do all the things we teach in this book, and you'll have a sound relationship. It makes sense to me that when people get what they need from their relationship—mostly a feeling they are loved—they don't stray.

Another Perspective

There have been other times in our marriage when we've been out, and men are talking to me—maybe they are flirting with me, and maybe I'm flirting back—and Paddy gets jealous and angry. I remember one night in particular when I met a man on the dance floor who had the same medical condition as I do and I ended up spending over an hour talking to him. It wasn't flirtatious in my opinion, and we exchanged some interesting information, but Paddy was furious. I honestly did not (do not) understand why on earth he would feel that way.

Here is my perspective on those types of situations: I've watched Paddy flirt with other women, and I've watched women fall all over themselves trying to impress Paddy. I get some enjoyment from watching these scenes go down. Flirting is fun, and I can see Paddy is having fun! When women are all over Paddy, it boosts his confidence, which is sexy to me. I say, flirt away!

The way I see it is that it has nothing to do with me. I'm not naïve enough to think Paddy will never be attracted to someone else—there are millions of hot, fun, smart women out there. I'm also not naïve enough to think Paddy won't ever think or even fantasize about other women—a previous lover, someone he's met, or even an imaginary one. I fully expect him to be attracted to other women and be attractive to other women, too. It's natural; it is how men are built, and doesn't have anything to do with our relationship or me.

Those feelings (which we cannot control, only our actions) are not a violation of the feelings we have for each other unless he decides to act on them and he would have to act on them in a fairly significant way before I felt threatened. Instead, I feel proud to be the one going home with him and if I did feel threatened in any way (this has yet to happen) I think I would move in on the situation. I would go lay a big wet kiss on him, grab his ass, and join his conversation. Since I feel this way, I expect everyone to feel this way.

I've found out I'm in the minority on jealousy. When I describe this to people, they usually say, "Oh, that's because you've never had anyone cheat on you." Not true. My first love from high school, my boyfriend on and off for three years, cheated on me. It did make me feel sick, and I threw up (but it turned out I had the stomach flu, so I'm unclear as to whether this was jealousy or not).

Maybe consider changing your thinking? I've never lost any sleep over jealousy and, from what Paddy has told me about how it feels, I'm pretty glad I haven't.

CHAPTER 11

GRATITUDE AND FORGIVENESS

Gratitude, forgiveness, and love all go hand in hand in hand. You won't ever find Pragma if you don't learn how to feel and express all of these. This goes foremost for loving yourself because it's the most effective way you can carry it over to loving others. While gratitude can be a way of showing appreciation for your partner, we believe it goes much deeper than that.

HE SAID: THE GATEWAY TO LOVING

Along with loving yourself, being grateful is essentially the gateway to loving. By showing gratitude and saying the words to each other and ourselves, we are expressing love. The more gratitude we show for all that is around us, the closer we get to experiencing total Agape love. (All loving, like Buddha and Jesus, remember?) The easiest place to practice gratitude is to be grateful for your loved ones and all they do.

Gratitude, when applied to your partner, is a daily reminder of why you love them. It may sound silly as most of us would not say we need a daily reminder. Why would we? This person is the love of my life! Boom! Enough said! But there are many other reasons we love one another and gratitude is the easiest way to acknowledge, remember, and appreciate the little things AND the big stuff. And most of us don't do enough of it.

The Little Things

In a relationship, many things get done that benefit all parties. These are things partners do FOR themselves AND each other. Going to work every day, wheeling, dealing, and making things happen are all things we do to succeed, and that ultimately benefit the whole family. So is doing a load of laundry, going to the bank, grocery shopping, and about a thousand other little things that have to get done. In a perfect world, everything would be equal; all chores, all income and all household administrative work would split right down the middle. We can dream. But the only real way to balance the inequity is to express massive amounts of gratitude for time spent devoted to a team function.

Be grateful for your partner and all they do; it is critical in your relationship. No one task can be looked on as more important than another when it comes to gratitude. You are either grateful for it, or you are not.

By being grateful for it, you elevate its importance at that moment and acknowledge your partner for it. You show your partner love for doing what they do. It helps us to keep doing it. How many times have you heard "Why should I? No one seems to care." That is just indifference, trained by a lack of gratitude. If we express heartfelt gratitude for all we do for each other, that indifference can't exist.

The BIG Stuff

I am grateful for all that Sam is, not just what she does. When I focus on the things that I am grateful for in her, it is impossible for me to do anything but love her completely. If I concentrate on the things I love most about myself, there is less room for the judgy negativity. If I focus on what I love most about the world, there is less room for everything that is not right. Gratitude is the ultimate shit sweeper. The more you put out there, the less shit there is to see.

What is this Forgiveness You Speak of?

"It's called Irish Alzheimer's Disease; you forget everything except the grudge." A friend told me that once. It is mostly funny, but it also rang a bit true for me. Many times I didn't remember exactly why I didn't like or was mad at someone. I just knew I was.

Forgiveness is something I have learned much from Sam about. Learning about it and practicing it are two different things, however. It has taken me some time to get decent at forgiveness. I am getting better at forgiving others for past indiscretions and letting things go because of her help. And when it happens it is a huge weight off my shoulders that rarely comes back. So I do recognize how important it is for mental well-being.

Forgiving myself is a whole other can of worms. It goes back to self-love and being able to forgive yourself for lack of perfection. For me, that is fucking hard. But I try to do it every day and am happy to report that I am also getting better it. I told you in the beginning that I was far from perfecting self-love, but I do recognize how critical it is and how forgiveness is the key to its mastery.

SHE SAID: FORGIVENESS SAVED MY LIFE

I'm going to start with forgiveness. I will be honest and say I did not understand forgiveness until two years ago, but this realization of what forgiveness truly is has completely changed me and all of my relationships.

I thought forgiveness was something you granted to other people when they had apologized for their wrongdoings and were, well, *worthy* of it. Wrong, wrong, so very, very wrong.

Nelson Mandela is one of the most brilliant embodiments of forgiveness. Imprisoned for twenty-seven years for his work against apartheid in South Africa, he forgave everyone involved in his imprisonment as he walked out of the prison.

Using my definition of forgiveness, all of the people who imprisoned him—all of the people who kept him imprisoned and who mistreated him while he was in prison—they were not apologizing or asking for forgiveness, so the entire first step of my forgiveness process is completely missing! How can you forgive someone who isn't asking for (nor do they want) your forgiveness? Using my model, forgiveness is for the one being forgiven.

Forgiveness is not for the person or people you are forgiving. Forgiveness is for yourself. Nelson Mandela knew if he held onto all the negative feelings against his captors, he would still be imprisoned—emotionally.

I have been a grudge-holder most of my life. My dad was a grudge-holder, and he was my hero, so I became a grudge-holder too.

About a year after my dad died, I had a significant falling out with my mom and my sister. There was plenty of finger pointing and blame to go around without resolution. This was when my grudge against them began. After three years, this grudge-holding became more burdensome and painful than the things that had hurt me in the first place.

In my mind, they turned from being my close loved ones to my enemies. I spent lots of time and energy engaged in very negative thoughts and feelings towards them. As much as I wanted to amend my relationships with them on some level, there was no indication they felt the same way; they did not appear to care whether they had hurt me and they were not seeking my forgiveness. I spent lots of time also feeling sorry for myself. I felt rejected, unloved, and spent a ton of time wallowing in self-doubt and wondering what all must be wrong with me that I had become unworthy of their love. All of these things weighed on me so very heavily that I became not only depressed but was diagnosed with an anxiety disorder and developed debilitating panic attacks.

I wish I could tell you I figured out what needed to happen myself. It wasn't until I was going through that spiritual training class I mentioned earlier with Jenai Lane that I finally understood what forgiveness is and why it matters.

Holding those grudges was in not hurting my mom or sister for all I knew. I did know it was hurting me—and not just emotionally. It was now affecting my physical health in a tangible way. For me to heal myself, I needed to forgive. I needed to let go of what I felt was wrongdoings and forgive them. I also needed to forgive myself for whatever I had done as a part of this unfolding drama, even if I wasn't sure exactly what it was.

Forgiveness is letting go of all resentment, anger, and negativity for good.

Jenai has two brilliant tools for learning and practicing forgiveness. One is called "Let Go and Know," and the other is called "Forgive for Good." Both can be found in her book *Spirit Led Instead*. READ this book! It has many great tools in it—I've found them very helpful for increasing my emotional intelligence, self-knowledge, and well-being—not to mention my spirituality! Better yet, sign up for one of her many workshops or one-on-one coaching. You won't regret it.

I used these tools to really learn what forgiveness is and feels like and I practice the "Let Go and Know" tool every day so I don't forget!

Shifting to Gratitude

Spend some time getting rid of your emotional shit through forgiveness then spend some time putting in some positive emotions! Take a minute right now and either think of, say, or write ten things you are grateful for in your life.

If you took the time to do this, do you feel a little lighter, a bit happier, and more positive about things than before you made this list? Gratitude is a very special emotion that very quickly lifts us up. It helps us focus on all of the good things in our lives and on our strengths.

We have an acquaintance named John Berghoff who teaches something called Appreciative Inquiry[12]. It's a revolutionary method of helping organizations and systems to evolve to become their best and strongest. This approach starts by focusing on everything that is going WELL in the organization or system, unlike many other methods that center on solving problems.

---

12   http://www.lead2flourish.com/

The idea is to strengthen the strengths so much that the weaknesses are irrelevant. What if you could do this in your relationship?

The first step is to spend time fully appreciating your partner and your relationship. As Paddy mentioned, some of this gratitude may be for things your partner does. Some of it may be appreciation for your partner. Some may stem from what your relationship has allowed you, given you, taught you. It is a great exercise to foster feelings of deep love for your partner. You may have to go back to when you felt very loving towards your partner if you are in a place where you're finding it difficult to find the positive. But there is always something you can find that is positive about your partner.

What you focus on grows. When you choose to be grateful, you'll focus on all the positive things and strengths. Then they'll grow, and so will all of that positive energy gratitude generates!

The next step is to spend some time envisioning the picture of your ideal relationship! How do you spend your time together? What do you feel when you are together? How does your partner feel when you are together? How do things work in your household if you live together? What kind of activities do you do together to have fun? This is time for you to really think about what you want and need from a relationship.

A friend recently told me her parents, who've been married multiple decades, say the secret to their lasting relationship was having something to look forward to together. Take some time to design that thing to look forward to together—a loving, thriving, healthy relationship. Because that is what our goal is: to help each and every person who reads this book have the relationship of their dreams. Or even better, to have a relationship they never even dreamed possible.

CONCLUSION

We wish there were some quick fix or pill you could take to make your relationship so strong it will last as long as your life. We wish we could promise you a smooth sailing kind of love forever. We wish this book were full of easy answers. But if all those dreams came true, there'd be little opportunity for the transformative growth that so often comes from meaningful, long-term, committed relationships.

And that's what we've really been talking about this whole time, isn't it? This book is about transformation. It's about paradigm shifts. It's about developing some new habits and dropping some old ones. It's about change and not giving up even though you continue to stumble and make mistakes. It's about endeavor.

We believe the love bond you create with your significant other is one of the strongest bonds in the universe. If we can help strengthen that relationship and the love it is built around, then our first mission is accomplished.

We also believe there is a worldwide crisis. Love itself is under siege. If you turn on the news, it will take about two minutes to recognize the world needs more people who understand how to love and its greater purpose. You must begin with understanding and loving yourself.

Once that is accomplished, you will be the best equipped to share your love with others. Learning about love won't just help you in your relationship but, more importantly, it helps you understand what it means to love and love well, and how to give and receive love in healthy, powerful, resonant ways. The better all of us understand and implement this, the more we believe love will grow. If we can start a movement to increase love in a place as simple as our homes, then maybe it can extend to our neighborhoods, towns, cities, countries, and the crisis can be averted.

Bigger Love is a combination of our story, how we saved our relationship and what valuable tools we have picked up along the way. It doesn't have all the answers, and it is not a definitive book within its category (as no book really can be) but we hope that you will recognize and appreciate it for what we intended. That is a book written as a guideline and a tool that entices you to want to learn more.

If we can learn to love ourselves better, we will become much more accomplished at loving others. If we become more consistent and skilled at giving and receiving love, then maybe those who feel its warmth and see its great beauty will strive to spread that love. The more love we spread, the better the world becomes. We believe this is the meaning of life. We can't think of a better gift to give the world than love.

TAKE SOME L.E.A.P.S WITH YOUR RELATIONSHIP!!

5 Simple Steps to help you remember all our pearls of wisdom

L. Love yourself always

E. Express love to your significant other using patience and THEIR love language

A. Appreciate your significant other with gratitude and forgiveness

P. Presence- be present in the moment always. Turn off that damn phone and listen!

S. Sex! More of it! Just Say Yes!!

ACKNOWLEDGEMENTS

In the spirit of gratitude, we want to thank YOU! Thank you for reading this book. Our hats are off to your love endeavor! We would also be so very appreciative if you would join our Facebook page, Bigger Love Book, and share your favorite parts of the book as well as your stories, successes, ah-ha moments, issues, and challenges you've had or are having through your own love endeavors.

We want to thank our children, Jacob and Claire, for teaching us about love as no one else could. We want to thank our parents—Betty and Denny, Dale and Ed—whose long-lasting relationships have taught us so much.

We want to thank all of our friends who were willing to share their stories—both intentionally and unintentionally, named and unnamed—therefore helping make the book more interesting.

And a very special thank you to Dan Cullinane who has been our counsel in love since the beginning and who also provided his invaluable feedback through all of the versions of this book.

THE SELF LOVE WORKSHEETS

Do you love yourself? If you do love yourself, do you engage in self-loving behaviors?

ADDRESSING NEGATIVE SELF-TALK

Listen to what you say to yourself inside your head. What are some of the things you say to yourself that are not self-loving or are negative? List them below. (If you're not sure, take a day or two and really try to listen to your thoughts. What do you say to yourself throughout the day? How many of these messages are negative?)

_____

_____

_____

_____

_____

_____

_____

_____

_____

_____

_____

Now take a few deep breaths, close your eyes, and think of someone you love very deeply. Now imagine saying these things to them the same way you are saying them to yourself. How does that make you feel? This might prove to be heartbreaking if you fully engaged in this activity. Did you start to feel defensive, angry, or hurt?

The person you have the most responsibility to take care of on this planet is yourself. YOU are the one you love very deeply, desire to protect, would do anything for, and think of very highly. And the person speaking badly about this person, knocking them down through criticism and judgment is also you. You may also believe your self-talk. You think the criticism and judgment are justified. But think again about your loved one. Are those messages ever justified? Is that kind of treatment ever justified? Is it ever okay to knock someone down with negativity? You wouldn't let anyone else do that to your loved one, you wouldn't do that to someone else, so you have to stop doing it to yourself.

When your thoughts turn critical towards yourself, take a moment to stop and label the thought as being negative. Recognize this is JUST A THOUGHT—not truth—and this THOUGHT does not serve you. Forgive yourself immediately and move on.

The more you practice recognizing these thoughts as thoughts, not giving them any power and forgiving yourself, you'll see those thoughts come less and less and eventually you won't be saying them to yourself anymore!

IN LOVE TO LOVING WORKSHEETS

FIVE ACTIVITIES THAT FOSTER CONNECTION

The Zone

Have you ever become hyper-focused on one thing, so focused that you were in an almost meditative state, where you didn't have to think about what you were doing, it just happened? We actually have the ability to do that more than we know. It can even be done with our partners. Imagine being so focused, so in tune with your partner that you almost did not have to speak because you already know what the other will say or do.

Have you been there before? What else do you think you were focusing on when you were in that zone? It probably wasn't your job or a trip, or a project you want to do around the house. It was just you and your partner in that moment. I am going to go out on a limb and say that I bet that moment was a top-five moment in your relationship. So why not go there again? And again? It is hard, but not impossible. We can achieve hyper-focus if we really put in the effort to make it happen. Here is where I restate the theme of this book for the nth time: We just have to work at it!!

Wouldn't it be cool though, for you and your spouse

to take a night and do nothing but spend time together focusing on each other? Choose an evening in the next seven days where you remove all distractions from your lives and do something together. Just the two of you. No phones, no TVs, no friends or family. Just the two of you. The goal is to just be with each other. BE patient, BE present, BE loving, BE grateful ... Just BE. *Helpful tip: You may want to book a hotel room on this night as you will likely want to extend the evening for as long as possible.*

Stretch Your Legs

Make a schedule to go for a walk or hike or bike ride a few times a week. Don't make it so strenuous that you can't enjoy each other's company and chat along the way. Take the dog if you want but don't bring any phones. *Helpful Tip: We sometimes bring wine or beer in a cup if it's a walk or a bottle of Champagne if it's a hike. It makes for an excellent romantic toast when you get to the top!*

Take a Bath or Shower Together (HE SAID)

I love any exercise that involves getting naked. Taking a bath or shower with your partner is the best way to do that. Make sure you have enough time to be playful during and after. *Helpful Tip: Don't just stop at washing each other's backs!*

Gain Some Perspective (SHE SAID)

Sometimes watching other people like, admire, love, or have any other positive feelings towards your partner can bring those same emotions to the surface in YOU. When we first moved to Kansas City, we didn't have many friends. One of my fondest memories was when we came back to Utah for our Christmas vacation, and we went out with a bunch of Paddy's friends. As I watched him interact with people he was comfortable with, people who knew him really well and loved him, I fell back in love with him all over again! Those people helped me remember all the reasons I fell in love with Paddy in the first place and he was definitely at his best too, filled with joy and passion and love for those longtime friends. Sometimes you can just see your partner through another person's eyes—someone who adores them—and you can feel those same adoring feelings fill you up!

Co-Adventure

Find something of common interest that might push each other's comfort zones a bit. We recently took a couples trip where several couples swung together out of a gondola four hundred feet above a ravine. It was scary as hell, and we did it with our partners. It was an experience we won't ever forget. That may be a bit extreme for some, but there are many other things couples can do in this category. Here are some examples of things our friends have talked about that they did as a couple: running a marathon, running a 5k, diving with sharks, skydiving, climbing a BIG mountain, hiking parts of the Appalachian trail. Whatever the adventure, it is that much more special when you get to do it with the one you love the most.

PRACTICING GRATITUDE WORKSHEETS

Gratitude, as we mention in the Forgiveness & Gratitude chapter, is magical! It can quickly transform negativity to positivity. Another great way to build on your self-love is to practice gratitude. Let's start off easy. Make a list of at least ten things you are grateful for in your life (examples: your home, your children, clothes on your back, running hot water, laughter, etc.):

1.
2.
3.
4.
5.
6.
7.
8.
9.
10.

Now, since this is a book about relationships, let's make a list of at least ten things you are grateful for your partner for (check the Expressing Love chapter for examples):

1.
2.
3.

4.

5.

6.

7.

8.

9.

10.

Now for the challenge—and this is the most important bit: make a list of at least ten things you are grateful and appreciative of for yourself. (There are a couple of ways to come at this gratitude. There are your physical attributes—*I'm grateful for my body and my senses that allow me to experience our wonderful world!* There are your "gifts" or the things you're good at—*I'm grateful for my creativity and my songwriting. T*here are the things you value or are dedicated to—*I'm grateful for my dedication to my health. I'm grateful for the love I have for my partner.* This should get you started!)

1.

2.

3.

4.

5.

6.

7.

8.

9.

10.

Was this difficult? It is for most people. We ran a workshop with about twelve couples, and almost everyone complained this was not an easy exercise. I believe in our society we're not taught about healthy self-love; we're taught about negative and excessive forms of self-love like egotism and narcissism, but not how healthy self-love can benefit us, our lives, and our relationships. As you can see, this activity is not about bragging, arrogance, or conceit. It is about appreciating all the wonderful things about YOU!

Another good hack on this self-gratitude is to cheat and steal some of the items from your partner's list if you happen to be doing this together.

THE FINANCIAL SAME PAGE WORKSHEETS

Each of you needs a piece of paper and a writing utensil. Or, if you want to go digital, use your computers or phones. Go into separate rooms and make a list of your top five values—the things in your life you consider to be your highest priorities. Then also list your top five goals— the things you want most in your life.

Here is how our lists turned out:

SAM'S TOP 5 VALUES	PADDY'S TOP 5 VALUES
Paddy	Sam
Kids	Kids
Friends & Family	Continual Improvement of Self
Long-Term Financial Security	Philanthropy
Writing Music	World Travel

SAM'S TOP 5 GOALS	PADDY'S TOP 5 GOALS
Weekly date with Paddy	Sell software for more than XXMM
Annual trip w/each kid & one family trip	Visit every continent with Sam
Meaningful trips & experiences with friends & family	Donate over seven figures to charity
Financial freedom in 5 years or less	Ability to live part-time on the beach and part-time in the mountains
Release at least 3 full-length albums	Bucket list adventures for kids and parents

Now, from those lists, you can begin your discussions on what you will agree are your top five values as a couple and then your top five goals as a couple. This exercise helps you determine what things are most important to you both and creates a kind of hierarchy with regard to how you make decisions.

Here is what our joint lists look like. NOTICE that they are different from both of our individual lists! It took a number of hours of discussion to find our same page. These values and goals should be revisited at least annually, especially if you've had significant life changes!

SAM & PADDY'S TOP JOINT VALUES
Continual Improvement of Self (Spirit, Body, & Mind) SELF LOVE!
Each Other
Kids
Friends & Family
Long-Term Financial Security (Pays for philanthropy, writing music, & world travel)

SAM & PADDY'S TOP JOINT GOALS
Dedicating time & resources to improving ourselves and supporting each other in those journeys with a focus on health and well-being for longevity
Weekly date nights, annual couple's trip and spiritual retreat together
Annual family Christmas bucket-list vacation/trip with the kids, continuing to ask what love & support means for Jacob and Claire as they grow and change and doing THAT!

Continue to develop circles of quality friendships that help us grow, continuing to find ways to create intimacy within our family relationships and friendships (trips, meals, etc.), providing support as necessary
Sell software for more than XXMM, continuing to live beneath our means to maximize our investments

The next step is to narrow those down to your shared goals for the year. Here is where you drill down on each of those high-level joint goals and turn them into measurable goals with deadlines.

Here is where we ended up as an example. You can see that to make our goals specific, some of them are things we want to achieve separately but we've both agreed to support one another in achieving them. We know these things are the highest things on our priority lists.

SAM & PADDY'S JOINT GOALS 2017
Consistent exercise (5X per week), healthy anti-inflammatory diet (5X per week), daily meditation, learn Spanish, release 1st book (this one!), release 1st album, & one spiritual retreat
Weekly date nights, annual couple's trip (Belize), and spiritual retreat together (Theo)
Family Christmas trip to Mexico, one adventure with each kid w/Sam TBD, weekly visits/calls with kids, monthly dates with kids as long as we are in close enough proximity
Mastermind participation, 1Life Fully Lived conferences, Powell trip, monthly family dinners, overnights with nieces for their b-days, Paddy golf trip w/Mom, Sam monthly dates w/Mom
Create a revenue stream with the software, create & manage budget, invest $XXKK

NOW, keeping these goals in mind, take your financials to the ultimate level and build a financial plan. Include your budget, income minus expenses, and whether you are living beneath your means (which should always be your financial plan!!!), so you will have money left over to either pay down debt, invest, or reach your goals. We highly recommend putting together a budget and going through your financials AND these goals on a monthly basis to see how you're doing!

Made in the USA
Columbia, SC
18 December 2017